PLAINS STATES

JOB SEEKERS

SOURCEBOOK

The most complete and accurate source for fast access to the key contacts within the placement industry to help find a job, change careers, or promote yourself.

Donald D. Walker and Valerie A. Shipe

Net-Research
16731 East Iliff
Suite B-183
Aurora, Colorado 80013

JOB SEEKER'S SOURCE BOOK

The "Plains States", Copyright 1993 by Valerie A. Shipe and Donald D. Walker. Printed and bound in the United States of America. All rights reserved.

No part of this book may be reproduced in any form without the express permission in writing from the publisher, except by a reviewer, who may quote brief passages in a review.

Published by: NET-RESEARCH
16731 East Iliff
Suite B-183
Aurora, Colorado 80013

Cover Design by: Salvatore Concialdi

Disclaimer of All Warranties and Liabilities

Although the authors have exhaustively researched all sources to ensure the accuracy and completeness of the information contained in this book, we assume no responsibility for errors, omissions, inaccuracies, or any other inconsistencies herein. Any mistakes or slights against people or organizations are unintentional.

For information on distribution or quantity discount rates, contact: Net-Research at (303) 690-9430.

Distribution to the trade is by Independent Publishers Group.

To order copies of this or other SourceBooks, contact the Independent Publishers Group at: 1 (800) 888-4741

ISBN: 1-882499-10-7

Library of Congress Catalog Card Number: 93-23285

**PLAINS STATES
JOBSEEKERS SOURCEBOOK**

TABLE OF CONTENTS

ACKNOWLEDGEMENTS   V

DEDICATION   VII

1. **INTRO: JOB SEEKERS SOURCEBOOK**   1

    Getting the most out of this book -- A special note to employers -- Using this book effectively

2. **SPECIALTY CODES - GUIDEPOSTS FOR YOU**   7

    What are they -- How to use them efficiently -- Specialty Code Table -- Specialty Code Definitions

PLAINS STATES JOBSEEKERS SOURCEBOOK

3. **GUIDELINES TO A SUCCESSFUL JOB SEARCH**   17

   Organizing your job search -- Additional help getting started -- General preparation -- Creating the perfect resume -- Secrets to writing a cover letter -- Preparations before the interview -- Handling the interview -- Important questions to ask -- After the interview follow-up -- Stress management made easy -- How people find jobs

4. **EMPLOYMENT AGENCIES/RECRUITERS**   47

   What is an employment agency? -- How to select an employment agency -- Questions to ask to qualify a employment agency -- Working with an employment agency -- Questions to ask about job openings -- Topics you should not discuss with recruiters -- Recap

   ### Iowa Employment Agencies/Recruiters   57

   Index Cross Reference by Specialty -- Alphabetical list of Iowa employment agencies/recruiters

   ### Kansas Employment Agencies/Recruiters   81

   Index Cross Reference by Specialty -- Alphabetical list of Kansas employment agencies/recruiters

   ### Nebraska Employment Agencies/Recruiters   101

   Index Cross Reference by Specialty -- Alphabetical list of Nebraska employment agencies/recruiters

   ### North Dakota Employment Agencies/Recruiters   117

   Index Cross Reference by Specialty -- Alphabetical list of North Dakota employment agencies/recruiters

PLAINS STATES JOBSEEKERS SOURCEBOOK

South Dakota Employment Agencies/Recruiters   123

Index Cross Reference by Specialty -- Alphabetical list of South Dakota employment agencies/recruiters

5. **EXECUTIVE SEARCH FIRMS**   131

How executive recruiters differ from employment agencies -- How to select an executive recruiter -- Key questions to ask to qualify an executive recruiter -- Working with an executive recruiter -- Questions to ask about job openings -- Topics you should not discuss with executive recruiters -- Recap -- Index Cross Reference by Specialty -- Alphabetical list of Executive Recruiters

BONUS EXECUTIVE SEARCH SECTION   167

Index Cross Reference by Specialty -- Alphabetical list of a **National Selection** of Executive Recruiters

6. **DATABASE, NETWORK, REFERRAL SERVICES**   189

Overview -- How to select a database, network, referral service -- Questions to ask to qualify a service -- Using a database, network, or referral Service -- Recap -- Alphabetical list of Database, Network, Referral Services

7. CAREER CONSULTANTS — 213

Consultant services, What are they? -- How to select the right career consultant -- Questions to ask to qualify a career consultant -- Working with a career consultant -- Recap -- Alphabetical list of Career Consultants

8. OUTPLACEMENT SERVICES — 231

A definition of Outplacement Services -- How to select the right outplacement service -- Questions to ask to qualify an outplacement service -- Working with a outplacement service -- Recap -- Alphabetical list of Outplacement Services

9. RESUME PREPARATION SERVICES — 243

Resume preparation services, How they differ -- How to select a resume preparation service -- Questions to ask to qualify a resume preparation service -- Working with a resume preparation service -- Recap -- Alphabetical list of Resume Preparation Services

CONTACT LOG FORMS — 269

Placement Firm Contact Form -- Hiring Company Contact Form

READER FEEDBACK FORM — 271

CATALOG OF NET-RESEARCH BOOKS — 273

ACKNOWLEDGEMENTS

This book could not have been produced without the dedication and cooperation of several people. In the months that it took to research and write this book, Val Shipe and I along with our research team contacted thousands of businesses to create the database of information included.

Many firms listed inside this book were first contacted by telephone to obtain critical source information such as: contact names, current addresses, phone numbers, and specialty disciplines.

Then to double check the information gathered, a letter containing the proposed business listing was sent back to each business for confirmation. Using the results of these confirmation returns, we finally put our book in its final form.

Our special thanks to the many firms listed in this book for their contribution and cooperation in helping us make this book the most current source of information available to job seekers, hiring companies, and firms in the placement industry.

Without their cooperation, we would not have been able to provide you with this valuable book.

Additionally, we wish to acknowledge the countless organizations, companies, and individuals who offered ideas, information, and review comments. The Job Seekers SourceBook grew out of personal experiences - our own and that of others, which enabled us to recognize the need to provide this consolidated source of timely information that would be beneficial to job seekers, hiring companies, and members of the placement industry.

And finally, thanks to you, our readers who continue to share our books with others. We are glad that people have been found "The Job Seekers SourceBooks" helpful in making the job search process more productive.

We value the comments and advice given to us by our readers. To enable you to help us improve this book and help others, we have provided a Reader's Comment form at the back of the book. Please share your comments with us by using this form.

Donald D. Walker
October, 1993

DEDICATIONS

This book is dedicated to Ron & Ginger Pawlish whose long time friendship and support we treasure.

                                            Donald D. Walker
                                            Valerie A. Shipe
                                                    Author

This book is also dedicated to my youngest great nephew Robert J. Jurries who brings our whole family so much joy.

                                            Valerie A. Shipe
                                                    Author

                "Let another man praise thee,
                and not thine own mouth"

                        Proverbs: 27:2

IMPORTANT NEWS FOR THOSE JOB SEEKERS LOOKING FOR A JOB OUT-OF-STATE !!!

Net-Research produces regional Job Seekers SourceBooks for areas across the entire United States.

Other Job Seekers SourceBooks currently in print include:

> Boston & New England
> Chicago & Illinois
> Dallas & The South West
> L.A. & Southern California
> Mid-Atlantic
> Mountain States
> New York & New Jersey
> Northern Great Lakes
> Ohio Valley
> Pacific Northwest
> Southern Atlantic Coast

Future Job Seekers SourceBooks due out soon include:

> Southern States

Job Seekers SourceBooks are available at special quantity discounts for bulk purchases for sales promotions, premiums, or fund raising.

For details, contact the Vice President of Special Sales, Net-Research, 16731 East Iliff, Suite B-183, Aurora, Colorado 80013

x

PLAINS STATES JOB SEEKERS SOURCEBOOK

Section 1

Getting The Most Out Of This Book

Welcome

Introducing:

The "Plains States Job Seekers SourceBook"!

IMPORTANT !!!

For the most effective use of your time, read this section first prior to attempting to use the materials contained within this book.

This book has been especially prepared for the individual who has decided to look for a new job. Unlike other books which provide lists of placement firms and related services, this source book provides detailed information to give you **fast** and **direct** access to organizations that can do you the most good.

Recognizing the frustration of trying to find the right resources for your job search, we have created the most comprehensive regional source listing of employment agencies, recruiters, executive search firms, database services, career consultants, outplacement services, and resume preparation services in the United States.

Proper use of this book will enable you to pinpoint the right organization for your particular needs. It contains services and helpful hints to aid everyone from entry-level to CEO, and covers virtually every field and profession.

Turn the pages and you'll find useful information about developing the most effective resume or cover letter, perfecting interview techniques and getting your foot in the door of a new career. This book will help you find the right contacts to aid in your personal marketing strategy.

Whether you are just beginning your job search or if you've been pounding the pavement for a long time, you will find this book to be absolutely the best source of helpful information.

Introduction

Special note to employers:

<u>Whether expanding your business or in the middle of a reorganization, this book is indispensable to you!</u>

When in need of people with certain skills and qualifications, it is important to quickly find the placement professionals who specialize in particular fields.

The Job Seekers SourceBook helps you do just that.

With the information contained within this book, you can quickly and accurately reference resources by specialty and location to improve the effectiveness of your match.

The Job Seekers SourceBook provides the most up-to-date and complete regional list of placement firms for use by hiring companies.

Every entry has been verified by phone and/or mail to ensure that you have the right tool at your finger tips to save you time.

During the difficult times of a reorganization, the Job Seekers SourceBooks provide your Human Resource departments with the best tool to help your former employees find a new job elsewhere.

Companies that provide their former employees with free copies of this book as part of an outplacement package have found that they have been able to help these people find jobs sooner.

How to use this Book

This book contains the most comprehensive listing of employment agencies, executive search firms, specialty recruiters, outplacement firms, career counselors, resume preparation firms, and database/referral services. Altogether there are over **900** listings in this book, all of them verified as to type of business and as to being active in business.

This book is designed to be user-friendly. Throughout the book, we have listed firms in alphabetical order and categorized them as to type of firm. In addition, employment agencies and recruiters have been separated into distinct geographic areas: Iowa, Kansas, Nebraska, North Dakota and South Dakota-plus a bonus section with selected search firms from across the nation. We have also provided vital identifying information with each listing to help make your job search easier.

The first section of the book is devoted to guidelines for a successful job search. Included are tips for interviewing, resume preparation, better writing, stress management, networking and overall preparation for your job search. Each topic is designed in an easy to read outline format that makes quick reference easier when the need arises.

The remaining sections cover the different types of firms functioning in the placement industry. Each section contains several pages of introduction which is filled with information designed to educate the reader on the type of firms listed and how to find and use these firms for maximum benefit.

Introduction

Following each introduction (where appropriate) is a cross reference by specialty to that section's list of resources that may be beneficial to your search. All businesses contained in the cross reference are then listed in alphabetical order for ease of access. Under each listing you will find the organization's specialty, the type of positions and clients they serve, and other pertinent information.

To maximize the benefit of using this book, first read the section titled "Guidelines to a Successful Job Search".

Next read the introduction to each of the other sections to determine which types of firms you will need to use in your job search.

Finally, review the Section of this book on Specialty Codes to familiarize yourself with the different industry fields and disciplines prior to selecting any firm for use.

Practical examples are presented in the Specialty Codes Section to quickly guide you to only those firms that you need to contact.

The goal of this book is to provide you with the right information to focus your job search efforts for timely success.

<u>This can be best achieved by following the suggestions identified above on this page.</u>

Good luck, and we hope you find this book a most valuable tool to assist you in finding a new career opportunity.

Important Job Hunting Fact

Two thirds of all job hunters spend five hours or less a week on their job search.

To be successful in your job search, work full-time on your search, spend at least 30 hours per week on this task.

PLAINS STATES JOB SEEKERS SOURCEBOOK

Section 2

Specialty Codes

What are they?

Specialty codes within this book are the identifying codes which enable the reader to quickly find those employment agencies, recruiters or executive recruiters that can be most helpful during a job search.

The full definition of specialty codes by industry disciplines and types of positions is contained within this section on the pages that follow.

Within this book every business listed in the sections for employment agencies/recruiters or executive recruiters has been tagged with one or more specialty codes based upon the information we have gathered.

The Index Cross References by Specialty Codes provide the reader with quick access to those firms that should be contacted first when conducting a job search.

How to use them!

If for example, you were in computer programming, then you would scan our list of specialty code definitions, until you found "C" for computers.

Reading the definition associated with this code you would see that one of the positions handled by firms that deal in area is that of computer programmer.

Knowing that your salary level is less than $70,000, you would next look to find those firms in the sections for "Employment Agencies Recruiters" that were tagged with this code.

The easiest way to do this is use the Index Cross Reference for one of these sections and scan down until you found firms listed under the heading: "Specialty C: Computers & Data Processing", which would appear like this:

Specialty: C
(Computers & Data Processing)

Business Management Personnel
Computer Futures Exchange Inc   <----If you selected this entry
Data Career Center   then you would scan the
Data Resource Consultants   alphabetical list until
                                                                    you found that entry.

(You would have found this entry)

Rick Ceater, Pres
Computer Futures Exchange Inc
727 N Hudson Ave, Ste 3
Chicago, IL 60610
(312) 951-0102
Specialty: C
Employment Agency

Reviewing this entry, you now have the contact name of who to call or write, the correct phone number and address, and the knowledge that this firm **only** specializes in placements within the computer industry since that is the only Specialty Code listed for this entry.

To maximize your efforts, always contact those firms first that deal exclusively in placements within your industry or discipline. Read the Introduction to each section to learn how to evaluate and locate the best firms to use in your job search.

SPECIALTY CODE TABLE

A	-	ADVERTISING
B	-	BANKING
C	-	COMPUTERS & DATA PROCESSING
E	-	ENGINEERING
F	-	FINANCE & ACCOUNTING
G	-	GENERAL APPLICATIONS
H	-	HEALTH CARE
I	-	INSURANCE
L	-	LEGAL
M	-	MANUFACTURING
O	-	OFFICE ADMINISTRATION
P	-	PERSONNEL & HUMAN RESOURCES
R	-	RESEARCH & DEVELOPMENT
S	-	SALES & MARKETING
T	-	TRAVEL, FOOD & HOSPITALITY

Specialty codes identify the specific industry areas that are served by Employment Agencies, Recruiters, or Executive Search firms.

SPECIALTY CODE DEFINITIONS

A - ADVERTISING

Disciplines: Advertising

Positions: Administrative Assistant, Advertising Worker, Media Specialist, Receptionist, Secretary, Typist, Word Processor

B - BANKING

Disciplines: Auditing, bookkeeping, branch management, consulting, financial analysis, loan processing/origination, operations management

Positions: Bank Officer, Branch Manager, Clerk, Credit Manager, Customer Service Representative, Data Entry Clerk, Loan Processor, Receptionist, Secretary, Teller, Trust Officer, Word Processing Specialist

C - COMPUTERS & DATA PROCESSING

Disciplines: EDP audit, programming, systems development

Positions: Computer Operator, Data Entry Clerk, LAN Specialist, MIS Specialist, Programmer, Software Engineer, Systems Analyst, Systems Programmer, Technical Writer, Telecommunication Specialist

SPECIALTY CODE DEFINITIONS

E - ENGINEERING

Disciplines: Aeronautical, chemical, civil, electrical, environmental/hazardouswaste, HVAC, industrial, manufacturing, mechanical, nuclear, & packaging

Positions: Architectural Engineer, Biochemical Engineer, Ceramics Engineer, Chemical Engineer, Civil Engineer, Construction Engineer, Electrical Engineer, Environmental Engineer, HVAC Engineer, Industrial Engineer, Mechanical Engineer, Metallurgical Engineer, Mining Engineer, Nuclear Engineer, Plastic Engineer, Petroleum Engineer

F - FINANCE & ACCOUNTING

Disciplines: Auditing, bookkeeping, commodities broker, budgeting, consulting, financial analysis, public accounting, tax accounting

Positions: Accountant, A/P Clerk, A/R Clerk, Auditor, CFO, Controller, Cost Accountant, Payroll Clerk, Tax Accountant

G - GENERAL APPLICATIONS

Disciplines: No specialty implied, usually used for entry level support, staff office worker/clerical, mid-level management, mid-level professional/technical

Positions: All general support positions

SPECIALTY CODE DEFINITIONS

H - **HEALTH CARE**

Disciplines: Dental, Nursing, Pharmaceuticals

Positions: Dental Assistant, Medical Secretary, Nurse, Receptionist

I - **INSURANCE**

Disciplines: Actuarial, Claims, Life/Health, Property/Casualty, Rating, Reinsurance, Underwriting

Positions: Actuary, Claims Adjuster, Clerk, Insurance Agent, Receptionist, Secretary, Underwriter

L - **LEGAL**

Disciplines: Legal

Positions: Attorney, Court Recorder, Legal Administrator, Legal Secretary, Paralegals, Receptionist

SPECIALTY CODE DEFINITIONS

M - MANUFACTURING

Disciplines: Factory automation, logistics, manufacturing/production, plant management, quality control, robotics, safety, supervisory, textiles, traffic management

Positions: Factory Worker, General Manager, Inventory Controller, Personnel & Labor Relations Specialist, Production Manager, Purchasing Agent, Quality Control Supervisor, Shift Supervisor, Traffic Manager, Warehouse Manager

O - OFFICE ADMINISTRATION

Disciplines: Administrators, clerks, management, receptionists, secretaries, supervisors

Positions: Clerk, Data Entry Clerk, Customer Service Representative, Legal Secretary, Medical Secretary, Office Manager, Office Worker, Secretary, Stenographer, Technical Writer/Editor, Typist, Word Processing Specialist

P - PERSONNEL/HUMAN RESOURCES

Disciplines: Personnel, Human Resources

Positions: Benefits Coordinator, Human Resources Manager, Payroll Administrator, Personnel Director, Personnel & Labor Relations Specialist

SPECIALTY CODE DEFINITIONS

R - RESEARCH & DEVELOPMENT

Disciplines: Product development, R&D, sales, technicians

Positions: Product Developer, Project Manager, Quality Control Specialist, Technical Writer/Editor

S - SALES & MARKETING

Disciplines: Business products, computers, consumer products, industrial products, real estate, retail, services/intangibles, trainees

Positions: Customer Service Representative, Marketing Specialist, Public Relations Specialist, Regional Manager, Sales Manager, Sales Representative, Sales Trainee

T - TRAVEL

Disciplines: Airlines, Hospitality, Hotel, Restaurant, Travel Agencies

Positions: Assistant Manager, Chef, Cook, Front Desk Clerk, Hotel Manager, Reservation Agent, Ticket Agent

SPECIALTY CODE DEFINITIONS

OTHER SPECIFIC SPECIALTIES

Where a particular specialty does not fit into any of the above classifications, it is listed as a specific specialty and placed in alphabetical order under a general category titled "Other Specific Specialties".

PLAINS STATES JOB SEEKERS SOURCEBOOK

Section 3

Guidelines to a Successful Job Search

Organizing Your Job Search

Getting organized for your job search is the most critical step you can take in finding the right position in the least amount of time.

Finding a job is kind of like solving a detective novel mystery. There are certain predefined activities that must be performed before the mystery can be solved. In the case of a job search these activities involve the following:

1. *Identifying sources for leads*

    Be creative in your thinking about possible source of job leads. Some good possibilities often overlooked by job seekers include: equipment manufacturers, special interest publications, trade publications, service directories, manufacturer's directories, books, and business newspapers.

    Take note of announcements about a company moving into the area, acquiring another company, or expanding its product line. All are potential sources for new job openings. Write down everything and keep track of it.

2. *Fill in the blanks*

   Once you have identified a lead, then spend the time to gather supporting information such as: contact names (include department heads), type of company, addresses, phone numbers, company size, growth potential and stability.

3. *Probe for information on openings*

   Find out who is in charge, then call and get an answer as to whether they have any openings now or in the future. Using an indirect approach such as: "Where can I put my knowledge of telemarketing to work?" often will help you obtain the best information about possible openings and who else to contact.

4. *Follow up on any openings*

   Once you've found where an opening is available, contact the individual in charge to request permission to send them a copy of your resume. Now is the time to do some advance selling of yourself over the telephone. If you found out about an opening through your own search efforts, then don't forget to sell them on your creative ingenuity as one of your skills.

   Include a carefully tailored and targeted cover letter that highlights how some of your key skills could be beneficial to this company.

   Tell them why they should hire you and not someone else...in one paragraph. Be creative and positive in your approach.

5. *Follow up your mailing*

   Allow a reasonable amount of time for your letter and resume to arrive, then call the company contact. Make this call to find out if there is further interest on their part and to schedule a convenient time for a personal interview.

   If there is no interest on their part, then probe to find out why. This is very important. You may find out that their objection has to do with experience or skills not listed on your resume. If so, then cover this on the phone to overcome their objections.

   Remember, the purpose of this follow up call is to validate their interest, overcome any objections, and to set a time for a personal interview.

6. *Attending the interview*

   Smile, and go into the interview with a positive attitude. Make that first impression of you a pleasant experience, because people like to be around pleasant people.

   No matter how badly you may need a job, never, never appear desperate.

   Appear confident without appearing arrogant. Remember, you know more about yourself and your previous job history than they do.

   Be prepared, review our guidelines titled: "The Interview".

   Take notes during the interview on key points, especially on any information that you promise to get back to them.

Audition for the part, sell yourself without being overbearing. Demonstrate why they should hire you. Relate your skills and experience to their needs.

After you have identified all of the reasons why they should hire you, then ask for the job. Too often, job seekers give a perfect sales pitch, then forget to close the sale by asking for the job.

If they're not ready to make a decision, then find out when the decision will be made and where you fit in the running. Mark this date down and follow up later with a letter and a phone call.

7. *Critique your interview*

   Immediately after the interview, identify what was good and what needs changing, then improve those areas that need to be better.

8. *One more time*

   Now is the opportunity to put your name in front of the interviewer again. Send out a thank you letter, recap how your background can be beneficial to their company, and ask for the job...one more time.

9. *Move forward and re-loop*

   Repeat your efforts as a good detective, and continue through this process again with other job leads.

   Persistence and perseverance will prevail.

Maintain a positive mental attitude and learn from any rejection.

Only by using the experience gained from each interview can you polish your performance.

Remember, by being better prepared than the other people applying for the same position, your opportunity of being selected as the right match is greater, which would result in you soon having the job you want.

Additional Help Getting Started

To assist you in being better prepared to conduct your successful job search, we have provided a set of useful guidelines on the next few pages of this book.

These guidelines are designed to help you handle the important aspects of your job search. They contain information on:

- General preparation needed prior to starting a job search.

- Instructions for creating the perfect resume.

- Cover letter creation for responding to job openings.

- The Interview Process (Before/During/After).

- Stress management during your job search.

- An overview of how people find jobs.

It is recommended that you read and follow them carefully.

Keep the faith, stay positive, and happy sleuthing.

General Preparation

1) If you are unemployed now, obtain some business cards that have your name, address and specialty listed. Hand these out to everyone you meet in your efforts to obtain employment.

   One of the best cards I've seen used by a job seeker had in large bold type, right in the middle of the card, the words: **"Between Successes"**. I contacted that person and interviewed him just because of the ingenuity displayed with this phrase.

2) If you want to relocate, check the job market in the area by reading local newspapers or information from the Bureau of Labor Statistics. Try to arrange and coordinate multiple interviews during trips to this new area to cut expenses.

3) Maintain a contact file with names, companies, titles, addresses, phone numbers, etc.

4) Attend job fairs, seminars, meetings, lectures, etc. and introduce yourself to as many people as possible.

5) Contact everyone you can to tell them you are looking. Explain the kind of job you are looking for and the two or three things that you do very well.

6) Try sending out broadcast letters to companies where you'd like to work (expect responses from about 20%, interview opportunities from less than 5%).

7) Find a mentor in your field and cultivate a relationship.

8) Be truthful in your interviews and on your resume/application.

9) Work on small talk.

10) Periodically evaluate your progress to maximize your results.

Creating The Perfect Resume

Think before you write

1) Make a list of your skills, honors, professional/civic organizations, languages, etc.

2) Assemble a list of past jobs with employers' names, addresses, phone numbers, dates that you started, supervisors' names and starting and ending salaries. Different jobs for the same company count.

3) Arrange the information on your resume so that your strongest points are near the top.

4) Jot down brief examples of what you accomplished at each job. Include actions you took and the results produced, showing increases in dollars, percentages and units wherever possible.

5) Identify people you want to use as references. Contact each potential reference to insure that they are aware of your job search and your intentions.

6) Determine what you do best and the kind of job you want.

Structure your resume

1) Think about your reader -- who will receive it and what is it going to tell them?

2) Head the resume with your name, address and phone number(s).

3) Make a single statement that identifies your capabilities and/or your job objective.

4) Use your past accomplishments to demonstrate your ability and experience for handling the new job.

   - Show jobs held, what was done and results achieved.
   - Strengthen the listing with chronological dates.
   - Be accurate.

5) Identify educational background -- especially as it supports your job objective.

6) Support with a list of skills, languages, honors or activities as they apply.

7) Edit for length -- one page if possible, two pages maximum.

Review your work

1) Check spelling, grammar, etc.

2) Avoid clutter -- the resume should give the reader a taste of your capabilities while leaving him or her wanting to know more.

3) Never use abbreviations.

4) Start sentences with verbs -- never use "I...".

5) When providing references, print them on a separate sheet.

6) Choose tasteful, business-like colors for paper and ink (white, ivory, light blue or gray are best for paper).

7) Limit your creativity unless the position you want warrants it.

8). Always keep your resume up-to-date. You never know when you'll need it.

Writing The Cover Letter

1) Prepare each cover letter as a unique personal response to a specific job opportunity.

2) DO NOT use form letters to respond to a job opening.

3) Match your background to the specific needs of the job opportunity.

4) Keep the cover letter brief and to the point, with no more than 3-4 short paragraphs.

5) Avoid long rambling sentences and abbreviations.

6) Ensure that the company and the person's name to whom the letter is being sent are spelled correctly.

7) Check each letter for spelling, grammar, and typo's.

8) Put your name address and phone number(s) on the letter.

9) Be courteous and truthful.

10) Ask for the opportunity of a personal interview to discuss your background and their needs in greater detail.

11) Choose tasteful business-like colors for the paper.

12) Use a heavy quality bond paper for your letters.

Preparations Before The Interview

1) Know who you are, not what you are.

2) Research the company, position and industry by:
   - going to the library
   - reading newspapers, magazines, etc.
   - calling or writing the company and asking them to send you information (annual report)
   - visit the company and ask for information (you might even get an informal interview)

3) Ensure that you have specific directions as to how to get to the interview location. Plan out your travel route, be aware of road construction and traffic patterns in the area.

4) Allow plenty of travel time to reach the interview location. Remember it is better to be there early than to be late. Use spare time to review your notes and check your appearance.

5) Write out a personal inventory of your strongest skills, areas of knowledge and personality traits, including goals and areas of improvement.

6) Prepare examples of past accomplishments with solid evidence of results achieved.

7) Practice a mock interview with a friend or spouse beforehand.

8) Prepare answers to tough questions you anticipate being asked -- especially ones that require comment on your negative traits. Make the response positive.

8) Make a list of past employers, addresses, phone numbers and job responsibilities -- to be able to fill out an application.

9) Check the weather forecast, and dress appropriately.

Handling The Interview

1) Dress appropriately and be well-groomed.

2) Don't eat, chew gum, smoke or drink during the interview.

3) Be polite, on-time and interested.

4) Prepare yourself ahead of time for possible questions.

5) Answer questions succinctly but completely.

6) Be honest about while you are looking for another job, but don't bad mouth you current or previous employer.

7) Ask pertinent questions about the job. You want to know as much about them as they do about you.

8) Remain calm. Many interviewers are more nervous than you.

9) Make good eye contact with the interviewer but don't stare.

10) If a tough question comes up, compose yourself before answering. The interviewer will respect your thoughtfulness.

11) Turn negatives into positives.

12) Keep smiling and sound pleasant.

13) Illustrate points with examples but don't ramble.

14) Bring extra copies of resume, references or samples of work.

15) DO NOT ask about salary, vacation time, etc.

16) Ask to take home a copy of the annual report or other company literature.

17) Be aware of your rights -- employers are not allowed to ask about creed, nationality, race, marital status, family plans or age, nor are they allowed to request a photo of you.

18) When asked about previous salary, be specific as to what you were making and what your benefit package was.

19) If asked what salary you are looking for, inquire as to what is the salary range of the position offered. If less then what you were making, you may want to adjust your requirements to fit their range.

This can best be done by telling them that an offer in this range taking into consideration your experience and positive attitude would be acceptable.

Your willingness to accommodate their needs and accept an offer of less than what you were making should be explained by the fact that you believe your future performance with the company will quickly be recognized and rewarded.

20) Don't forget to thank the interviewer for his or her time.

21) Ask for a business card from the interviewer, this will be useful for your follow-up later.

22) Leave one of your own business cards with the interviewer. This is just another way to reinforce the memory of your visit with them.

23) Close by asking the interviewer for a candid evaluation of his/her thoughts about your opportunity of being considered for the position.

24) Set a specific date and time for follow up for further information or for when you can expect a decision.

Important Questions To Ask

Questions to ask about Hiring Companies:

1. What is the overall objective and goal of the company?

   It is important to know whether a company is concerned about growth and expansion or if the company is positioning itself for the possibility of a future takeover. If the latter is true, then job security make be shaky.

2. What is the industry ranking of the company? How has that changed from the previous year?

   If a company is improving in the industry ranking from one year to the next, then this is the right one to hitch your star to.

3. How profitable is the company? How has that changed from the previous year?

   A company that is growing in profitability or has some very good reasons for any downturns is a better place than one which is losing money. You want one that isn't worried about where the next nickel is coming from.

4. What has been the turnover rate of the current staff and management?

   Beware of any company that has a high turnover rate, you could be walking through a revolving door.

Questions to ask concerning a specific job:

1. What are the specific experience requirements?

   The more that you understand in advance the needs of a specific position, the better you will be able to draft a cover letter that is targeted to respond directly to those needs.

2. What are the educational requirements?

   Understanding the educational requirements will allow you to propose experience and training courses as an alternative to overcome any potential objections if you lack the appropriate credentials.

3. What is the reporting structure?

   Knowing the chain of command will give you a better understanding of internal opportunities for advancement.

4. What are the responsibilities associated with the position?

   Identifying the specific responsibilities of a position will give you a measure to gauge your own experience against the needs of the company. It will also give you some insight into how exciting you will find the job if it is offered to you.

5. Where is the job located?

   A simple question, but often the interview for a position is held in a location different from where the position is located. Knowing where the job is will permit you to determine how much travel is required and to weight that factor when evaluating a job opening.

6. What are the normal working hours?

   Another simple but important question that helps prevent misunderstanding if asked up front.

7. Is this a salaried or non-salaried position?

   If this is a non-salaried position, then you need to know what the potential is for overtime and what is the pay scale associated with overtime.

8. What is the long term grow opportunity for this position?

   Everyone likes to have a goal to work towards, and one of the best goals available for employees is the reward and recognition associated with advancement. Know up front what opportunities are available for top performers to avoid any let down later.

Questions to ask concerning a job offer:

1. What is the makeup of the benefit package?

    You need to understand not only what is in the benefit package but also who pays for what portion of these benefits.

2. What is the salary range tied to the position?

    If the salary offered is at the high end of the salary range for a position, then you will know to expect minimal salary increases unless you are promoted into another position.

3. How often will there be performance reviews?

    It nice to know how often a performance review is performed so that you can have frequent feedback concerning your performance.

4. What is the normal schedule for salary reviews?

    Performance reviews and salary reviews are not always performed on the same cycle. Therefore by obtaining this information, it will prevent you from making false assumptions that lead to disappointment at a later date.

5. When do they need expect you to come on board?

    This is important in case you have any special plans that would conflict with their needs, or for you to give your current employer sufficient notice.

6. When do they need your answer to their offer?

    If you are unsure about making a commitment, then at least obtain a breathing period of a day or two to consider your decision. Once you've made your decision, then stick with it.

After the Interview Follow-up

1) On the same day, send brief thank-you notes to everyone encountered that day (receptionists, secretaries, etc.)

2) Send a thank-you note to everyone who interviewed you.

3) End your note to the interviewer(s) by reiterating your interest in the company and the position.

4) Begin follow-up calls one week later, and inquire as to how the selection process is going.

5) Continue to interview at other companies -- don't wait by the phone after each one.

6) Work to get multiple job offers, you will put you in the driver's seat for negotiating salary and benefits.

Stress Management Made Easy!

1) For immediate relief, practice stress-controlling exercises:

   - Alternately contract and relax muscles, counting to 10 in between.

   - Take a long, warm shower or bath.

   - Visit a masseur or masseuse -- a one hour session costs little more than a good haircut.

   - Exercise! It's amazing what sweat and sore muscles can do for improving your outlook.

   - Listen to soothing music in a quiet comfortable area.

2) Create a time-management plan and follow it.

3) Prioritize short- and long-term goals and write them down.

4) Create a financial planning strategy to project current expenses and anticipated expenses for the unemployed period.

5) Assess personal goals in relationship to the job market.

6) Talk with people -- you are not the only one looking for a job.

7) Keep things in perspective, remember that the man with no shoes is not nearly as bad off as the man with no feet.

8) Be easy on yourself and set realistic objectives.

9) Remember all problems have a definite life cycle, persistence will help you to shorten the time required to find a job.

10) Look in the mirror and smile, already you feel good.

How People Find Jobs

There is no sure-fire way to find your next job. It often seems as if luck, and being in the right place at the right time, have a lot to do with it. However, one thing is certain -- the more people you tell about your search for a new opportunity, the better your chance of finding it.

Here are some guidelines and facts for conducting your search:

Networking

- Call all friends and acquaintances, regardless of whether they are in your field or not

- Seek advice from them on finding a suitable job

- Identify 2-3 areas of expertise for them

- Query them for contacts to talk to for advice

- Ask if they will call ahead and introduce you

- Send these contacts a copy of your resume along with a cover letter that refers back to the contact source

- Follow up with a telephone call to determine interest and to establish a time for a personal interview

- Work new contacts for further leads to other potential jobs

<u>Employment Agencies
and
Recruiters</u>

- Are used more and more frequently to fill positions

- Cover specialized areas and fields

- Typically find people for jobs, not jobs for people

- Retain your information on file for only 6 months to a year

- Often control the best paying positions

- Require you to update information periodically

- Are most effective if they specialize in your field

- Often require the use of more than one firm for maximum exposure to the hiring market

- Require continue followup on your part to ensure that you remain an active presence

 Newspaper Ads

- Respond to ads quickly, within 2-3 days

- Provide a brief cover letter -- no more than 3-4 short paragraphs

- Tailor your resume or cover letter to fit the job description covered by the ad

- Beware of ads with only a phone number, P.O. Box number or ones that advertise false positions for job banks

- For maximum response, provide a self addressed, stamped postcard that provides check off boxes for ease of response.

    Examples of check off boxes:

    ___ Interested, will contact for an interview
    ___ Not a match at this time, will hold on file
    ___ Not Interested, however your resume will be routed for consideration to: _____
    ___ Not interested, however, send your resume to:
    _____
    _____
    _____

- For those jobs of particular interest, send a follow up letter after two weeks to keep your name fresh in their files

Database Services

- Growing in popularity -- used by many employment agencies

- Puts your job history in the hands of more people

- Provide a wider geographic exposure to the job market

- Can help employers find you sooner

- Retain your information on file for only 6 months to a year

- Require periodic information updating

- Access available from many sources such as resume preparation firms, employment agencies, private advertising, non-profit organizations, and college placement offices

- Available free or usually for a small fee

Videotaping Services

- Popular with companies for reducing travel/recruitment costs

- Save money and time, especially if you're planning to relocate

- Speed-up the selection process for hiring companies

- Can ease first-interview tensions

- Make in-person interviews more productive

- Provide wider geographic exposure to the job market

- Require a certain amount of front end preparation

- May require the payment of a small fee

- Provide the greatest flexibility of scheduling time for a screening interview

- On the down side, video interviews are often one shot deals performed at the request of the hiring company after they have received your resume.

Outplacement Firms/Employment Counselors

- Help to accurately evaluate your current skills

- Assist in matching your skills to a field or position

- Help you psychologically with the search process

- Aid in targeting the right hiring companies

- Require dedicated involvement on your part

- Effective in evaluating current job skills

- Assist you in organizing an effective job search process

- Provide an excellent support base

- Are most beneficial for those with special problems or skills

- Require the payment of a fee for services provided

- Are available on an hourly basis or a flat fee depending upon the type of services offered

Guidelines To A Successful Job Search

Resume Preparation Firms

- Help structure your resume to best suit a position sought

- Can be especially helpful when considering a career change

- Assist in creating and supporting an effective mail campaign

- Furnish the means of putting your job credentials in the best written presentation format

- Often provide access to resume database services

- Allow the easy creation of several specifically tailored resumes for emphasizing different job skills depending upon the position sought

- Provide a finished document which creates the best professional image for presenting your job history to potential employers

Job-Finding Facts

- 31.5% of jobs are found by applying directly to the employer
- 25% of jobs are found from networking with friends/relatives
- 12.5% of jobs are found through employment agencies
- 12.5% of jobs are found through newspaper advertisements
- 1.3% of jobs are found from union hiring halls
- 1.3% of jobs are found from civil service testing
- 16% of jobs are found through other methods

RECAP The key to finding a job can be found in this summary:

- Obtain and maintain a positive mental attitude.

- Get and stay organized.

- Always be over prepared for an interview.

- Use as many sources as possible to network.

- Follow up all leads and network for more.

- Pursue different avenues to obtain interviews and concentrate your efforts where responses are greatest.

- Remember, finding a job is work, to be successful, you must continually work at the process.

- Keep your sense of humor, even the worst problem looks better through a smile.

- Share with your spouse and family your concerns, it makes the burden smaller and easier to carry.

- Take time out to enjoy a nice day, smell the flowers, take a long walk, to recharges your energy level.

- When there appears to be nowhere else to turn, stop a minute, and pray, all things are possible with His help. Sometimes, we just forget to ask!

To quote the famous radio talk show host Bruce Williams, who I admire very much...

"I wish you well my friend".

PLAINS STATES
JOB SEEKERS SOURCEBOOK

Section 4

Employment Agencies/Recruiters

What is an employment agency?

Generally firms that place candidates in support and staff positions that pay $20,000 to $70,000 per year are called employment agencies, personnel consultants or recruiters. For purposes of grouping these firms in our source book, we use the label "Employment agency / Recruiter". For ease of reading this introduction, the terms "agency" and "recruiter" are used to refer to employment agencies/recruiters.

The value of an agency to a job seeker depends upon several things: the quality of the agency, the kind of work or position being sought, and your own level of experience. A good agency may help its candidates develop a strategy and prepare for personal interviews.

The benefit of an agency to a hiring company depends upon: the quality of the agency, the level of expertise contained by an agency's staff, the type of screening support performed by an agency to assist a company to quickly find the right person to meet its needs, and the span of individuals that are accessible to an agency from either the agency's own files or through its affiliations or network services.

Today many agencies are taking advantage of computer automation to share information with other agencies, making such agencies much more beneficial to both job seekers and hiring companies.

The next few pages contain important information on how to:

- Select an employment agency/recruiter to help you
- Work with an agency/recruiter

How To Select An Employment Agency/Recruiter

Finding the right employment agency or recruiter to help you find a job or change jobs requires some careful research on your part.

This is a process that cannot and should not be ignored. To maximize your chances of obtaining a job through this approach means that you must work hard to qualify and then select recruiters that you want to represent you in your job search. To assist you in this process we've outlined some important selection criteria that should be useful.

Selection Criteria:

The selection of the right firm to support your job search efforts should be based upon a combination of the following criteria:

Specialty — Does the firm specialize in making placements in your career field and industry?

If so, the firm is more likely to find you a new job. If it deals exclusively in your discipline, so much the better.

Experience — How long has the firm and the recruiter been in the placement business? And how long have they been making placements for members of your profession?

It is best to select a recruiter who has at least three years experience specializing in your industry. These recruiters will already have established a network of contacts with a number of hiring companies and will be better sources for job openings.

Proximity	Is the firm convenient for you to visit on a regular basis?
	Periodic office visits help you maintain high visibility with an individual recruiter.
Personality	Does the recruiter like you and do you the recruiter? Are you comfortable with the recruiter's business style and ability to represent you to hiring companies?
	If, yes, then you have a better shot at establishing and maintaining a good rapport with your recruiter on an ongoing basis.
Referrals	Was this agency referred to you by someone else in your field?
	Added to positive responses for the preceding qualifiers, a referral will give you an edge over other job seekers.
Quality	Does this agency have a good reputation and do they present themselves in a professional manner?
	The best way to determine this is to talk to other job seekers and to visit the recruiter's office to size them up. If you're unhappy with what you see or find, keep looking.
Networks	Is this recruiter or employment agency a member of a placement affiliation or shared database network?
	If yes, then the chances are better that having them represent you will give you broader exposure to a larger share of the employment market.

Questions to ask to qualify an employment agency/recruiter:

1. How long have they been in the placement business?

   The longer a firm has been in the business, the more contacts it is likely to have, therefore the odds of the firm being able to help you are better.

2. Do they specialize in making placements only in your career field?

   Usually, it is best to concentrate your efforts with just those recruiters that specialize in placing individuals with your background.

3. How many job openings are they working on at any one time?

   Typically ten to fifteen openings per month are good numbers for an individual recruiter.

4. How many placements do they average per month?

   Typically one to two placements per month are good numbers for an individual recruiter.

5. How many candidates are they working with?

   An average agency is likely to have three to four thousand resumes on file with maybe half of these representing people actively seeking new employment. Avoid those agencies that have more than 300 active candidates per agent, because you'll be easily forgotten.

6. How many client companies are they working with?

   Firms which average twenty companies per recruiter are about the right size to support you in your job search. Those below that level unless in a very narrow vertical market (ie. chemical engineers) or without a large number of annual job searches may not be active enough.

   Firms attempting to handle a larger number of hiring companies per agent may be spreading its resources too thin, especially if the number of placements per agent is low.

Working with an Employment Agency/Recruiter

Maximize your success of having an employment agency or recruiter find you a job, by remembering a few important axioms.

 Employment agencies or recruiters normally do not get paid until they place an individual into a fee paid position.

Therefore, do everything possible to help make their job easier. This includes having a very good resume available for their use and being prepared and on time for any job interviews that you agree upon.

 Employment agencies and recruiters will quickly lose interest in a job applicant that continually turns down job offers.

To prevent problems, be specific with the employment agency or recruiter as to what you are looking for in a company and a position. Do this during your first meeting with the recruiter.

If the job offer, the position, or the company environment isn't right, then by all means turn it down, but discuss it first with your recruiter so he/she understands your reasons. Just remember that you run the risk of losing support if you turn down too many offers.

 Employment agencies and recruiters prefer to have an exclusive commitment from a job seeker.

This means that if you are going to use multiple agencies or recruiters to speed up your job search, keep this information to yourself.

The level of interest an agency has in helping you find a job drops to almost zero once they know that you are shopping recruiters. There are more than enough job seekers out looking for a job that a recruiter hesitates to spend time on someone who any day may be placed through another agency. It could be a waste of both time and money to try to place that individual.

 Employment agencies and recruiters see as many as a hundred people each day. Also, an equal or greater amount of resumes are received in the daily mail from job seekers.

This means that you must get noticed and stay noticed, but this must be accomplished without becoming a pest. There are a variety of ways of doing this such as:

1. Hand deliver your resume to the firm and spend some time to ask questions, answer questions, and get a contact name.

2. Call on a weekly basis to update them on your status and to obtain an update from your recruiter.

3. Send a thank you note, right up front when a recruiter takes an interest in helping you.

4. Drop in the office once every two weeks to spend a few quick moments with your contact. Avoid Mondays or Fridays, as these days are always busy.

5. From time to time share a small gift (ie. donuts, candy, etc.) when you drop in for a visit.

6. When you come across current articles in newspapers or magazines about company expansions or relocations that could be beneficial to the recruiter, cut out the article and send it to recruiter along with a note.

 The service recruiters provide to job seekers is free, but don't abuse this service, recruiters need to make a living too.

Treat them with respect, and be thoughtful enough to at least notify them when you have taken a job offer from another source. If you really appreciated their efforts, send them a thank you card or a little gift to show your appreciation for their efforts.

If you were extremely satisfied with their efforts, refer job openings to them as well as other good job seekers. This will allow you to maintain contact with them and to keep your options open in case you need someone to again help you find a job in a timely manner.

 Recruiters know their job, but they don't know you or how well you can perform your job.

This means that they need your help in getting to know you. Remember, you know your job qualifications better than anyone, so tell them what you are good at. Describe and identify the important features of previous accomplishments. Furnish them with a means of measuring performance, such as a list of awards or reference letters.

Questions to ask recruiters about job openings:

1. How long has the job opening been available?

   If just a short time and you've received an offer, then this is a company that can make decisions quickly. If the job has been open a long time, then you need to know why, prior to making any acceptance decision.

2. Why is the job open?

   If someone retired or it's a new position, these are all positive signs. However, if someone has left the company or was terminated, then it would be nice to understand the circumstances before making a long term commitment.

3. When does a decision have to be made?

   Allow yourself some time to sleep on it before getting back to them. Be comfortable with your decision or don't do it.

4. How many people have already been presented?

   If a large number, than the odds are the hiring company has a backup candidate for the same job offer.

5. Why wasn't the position filled from within the company?

   If you don't like the answer, then the odds for future promotions within the company may be slim.

6. What is the long term opportunity for this position?

   Again, if you're looking for future growth, you need to be comfortable with the answer to this question.

Topics you should not discuss with recruiters:

1. Your knowledge about job openings in your field, until you have found and accepted a job yourself.

   Don't create unwanted competition for yourself.

2. Whether you are using other recruiters.

   To do so would reduce the interest in working with you.

RECAP

- If a placement firm doesn't have the experience in your field or the placement industry, it may not be the firm for you to use.

- If they don't handle a large number or the right type of hiring companies or if they have too many job seekers on file then they may be not be the best avenue for obtaining a job.

- Finally, if they do not handle a large number of job openings, especially in your field, then chances are slim they can be of any meaningful help to you.

Employment Agencies/Recruiters   57

Employment Agencies/Recruiters - Iowa

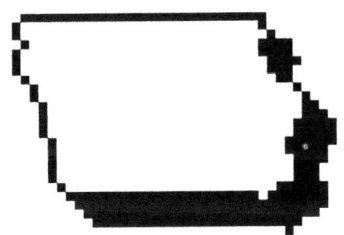

The following pages contain the specialty cross-reference listings to an alphabetical list of active employment agencies/recruiters located in Iowa.

The alphabetical listing is immediately after the cross-reference list.

INDEX CROSS REFERENCE BY SPECIALTY

Specialty: B
(Banking)

Bank Personnel Division
    of Personnel Inc
Banking Careers Ltd
Cambridge Permanent
    Employment
Key Employment Services
McGladrey Search Group
Robert Half International
The Williamson Group Inc

Specialty: C
(Computers & Data Processing)

Associate Personnel Inc
Cambridge Permanent
    Employment
Compu-Search
Deskins Technology
DP Search
Key Employment Services
McGladrey Search Group
Robert Half International
The Williamson Group Inc

Specialty: E
(Engineering)

Cambridge Permanent
    Employment
Key Employment Services
Mangement Recruiters

McGladrey Search Group
Mid-States Technical Staffing
    Services Inc
R Michael's & Associates Inc

Specialty: F
(Finance & Accounting)

Accountemps
Associate Personnel Inc
Cambridge Permanent
    Employment
Key Employment Services
McGladrey Search Group
Midtown Personnel
Robert Half International
The Williamson Group Inc

Specialty: G
(General Applications)

7000 Job Placement Ctr
A Professional Resume Svc
AAA Employment & Resume
    Specialists
Allen Resources
American Management
    Resources
Anders & Associates
BLR Associates
Brousseau Melissa & Associates
C S I Employment & Recruiting
Cafe Beaudelaire
Cambridge & Assocs Inc

Employment Agencies/Recruiters

Cambridge Temp Positions
Career Resources
CareerNet
Careers Inc
Careers Unlimited
Chenhall Personnel Services
City & National Employment
Corporate Suite Ltd
Dan Frommelt Personnel
Dee Springer Personnel
Employee Resources Inc
Employment Consultants
Employment Services Centers
Excel Employment Services
Executive Resources Ltd
Expertise Personnel Inc
Express Personnel Services
Express Services Temporary
Gadbury Temporary Employment
Hamilton Thomas
Help Inc
Human Resource Group
IA Comprehensive Human Service Inc
Insight Companies
Interim Personnel
Interstate Personnel Service
Iowa Job Service
Job Corps Applications & Placement
Job Market LTD Personnel Services
Job Service of Iowa
Job Training Area VII
Job Training Program
JTPA Area 8
Management Recruiters
Management Recruiters of Des Moines
Management Resource Group
McKirchy
Metro Temp
Murphy Employment Service & Co Inc
National Employment Wire Service
New Focus Inc
Oakstone Consulting
Off-Duty Police Services
Personnel Incorporated
Personnel Pool Temporary Svcs
Personnel Professionals
Pipeline Placement Ltd
Pratt Younglove
Preferred Personnel
Professional Placement
Project Assist
Proteus Employment
Proteus Employment Oprtnts Inc
Quality Recruiters Inc
Resource Placement Group III
Rhodes-Shanley & Associates
Rose Leonetti & Associates Inc
Rudy Salem Employment Agency
S E A R C H 21
Sac Co Outreach Center
Snelling & Snelling
Snelling Personnel Services
Spectrum Personnel Ltd
Spence Ewing & Associates
Staff Associates/Staff Temps
Strategicare Personnel Services
Tempro Services Inc
The Future Employment Service

Tucker Personnel Consultants
United Personnel Inc
Viall Nate & Associates
Weinstein S E Company
Western Temporary Svcs
Williams & Company
X-Pertise Personnel Inc

**Specialty: H
(Healthcare)**

Cambridge Permanent
    Employment
Execu Med Recruiters
Lee Smith & Associates
Mangement Recruiters
McGladrey Search Group
Medical Personnel Pool of Iowa
Midtown Personnel
National Healthcare Placement
    Assoc
Roth Young Personnel Services
The Williamson Group Inc

**Specialty: I
(Insurance)**

Key Employment Services
McGladrey Search Group
Mid American Search
Midtown Personnel
The Williamson Group Inc

**Specialty: L
(Legal)**

Midtown Personnel

**Specialty: M
(Manufacturing)**

R Michael's & Associates Inc

**Specialty: O
(Office Administration)**

Accountemps
Addtemps
ADIA The Employment People
Associate Personnel Inc
Cambridge Permanent
    Employment
Career Finders
Career Search Associates
Mangement Recruiters
McGladrey Search Group
Midtown Personnel
Office Mates 5
Pro-Tech of Des Moines Ltd
Staff Associates/Staff Temps

**Specialty: P
(Personnel/Human Resources)**

McGladrey Search Group
R Michael's & Associates Inc

Employment Agencies/Recruiters

Specialty: R
(Research & Development)

R Michael's & Associates Inc

Specialty: S
(Sales & Marketing)

Bryant Bureau
Cambridge Permanent
    Employment
Career Finders
Koster & Kompany
Lee Smith & Associates
Mangement Recruiters
McGladrey Search Group
Midtown Personnel
R Michael's & Associates Inc
Sales Consultants of
    Cedar Rapids
Sales Resources
Sales Search

Specialty: T
(Travel, Food & Hospitality)

Midtown Personnel
Roth Young Personnel Services

OTHER SPECIFIC
SPECIALTIES:

Specialty: Agricultural

Agra Placements Ltd

Specialty: Electronics

Midtown Personnel

Specialty: Food & Drug

Roth Young Personnel Services

Specialty: Industrial

Key Employment Services
The Williamson Group Inc

Specialty: Management/
Management Trainees

Career Finders
Key Employment Services
Staff Associates/Staff Temps

Specialty: Retail

Key Employment Services
Midtown Personnel
Roth Young Personnel Services
The Williamson Group Inc

Specialty: Supermarket

Roth Young Personnel Services

Specialty: Technical

Pro-Tech of Des Moines Ltd

Employment Agencies/Recruiters

Office Manager
7000 Job Placement Ctr
406 W Depot Ave
Fairfield, IA 52556
(515) 472-7837
Specialty: G
Employment Agency/Recruiter

Office Manager
A Professional Resume Svc
3009 Merle Hay Rd Ste 7
Des Moines, IA 50310
(515) 270-8442
Specialty: G
Employment Agency/Recruiter

Office Manager
**AAA Employment &
Resume Specialists**
2545 William Avenue
Sioux City, IA 51106
(712) 276-6517
Specialty: G
Employment Agency/Recruiter

Office Manager
Accountemps
317 6 Avenue Ste 700
Des Moines, IA 50304
(515) 282-8367
Specialty: F,O
Employment Agency/Recruiter

Office Manager
Addtemps
205 12th St SE
Cedar Rapids, IA 52403
(319) 362-3500
Specialty: O
Employment Agency/Recruiter

Office Manager
Addtemps
630 E Grand Ave Ste 1
Des Moines, IA 50309
(515) 244-3300
Specialty: O
Employment Agency/Recruiter

Office Manager
ADIA The Employment People
2600 Grand Ave Suite 114
Des Moines, IA 50312
(515) 243-2022
Specialty: O
Employment Agency/Recruiter

Office Manager
Agra Placements Ltd
4949 Pleasant St Ste 1
West Des Moines, IA 50265
(515) 225-6562
Specialty: Agricultural
Employment Agency/Recruiter

Office Manager
Allen Resources
1001 S Main St
Fairfield, IA 52556
(515) 472-9123
Specialty: G
Employment Agency/Recruiter

Office Manager
American Management Resources
3408 Woodland Avenue Ste 401
West Des Moines, IA 50266
(515) 222-9044
Specialty: G
Employment Agency/Recruiter

Office Manager
Anders & Associates
2500 18 Street
Bettendorf, IA 52722
(319) 359-9948
Specialty: G
Personnel Consultant/Recruiter

Joanne Hagedorn, Owner
Associate Personnel Inc
625 1st Avenue SE
Cedar Rapids, IA 52401-1315
(319) 362-3500
(319) 362-3321 FAX
Specialty: C,F,O,Temporary And Permanent Placement
Employment Agency/Recruiter

Joanne Hagedorn, Owner
Associate Personnel Inc
630 East Grand Avenue
Suite One
Des Moines, IA 50309
(515) 244-3300
(515) 244-3324 FAX
Specialty: C,F,O,Temporary & Permanent Placement
Employment Agency/Recruiter

Office Manager
Bank Personnel Division of Personnel Inc
516 Equitable Building
604 Locust Street
Des Moines, IA 50309
(515) 243-7687
Specialty: B
Employment Agency/Recruiter

Office Manager
Banking Careers Ltd
525 Merle Hay Tower
Des Moines, IA 50310
(515) 276-1151
Specialty: B
Employment Agency/Recruiter

Office Manager
Banking Careers Ltd
1300 Wall St
Webster City, IA 50595
(515) 832-1258
Specialty: B
Employment Agency/Recruiter

Employment Agencies/Recruiters

Office Manager
BLR Associates
P O Box 65967
West Des Moines, IA 50265
(515) 222-1989
Specialty: G
Employment Agency/Recruiter

Office Manager
Brousseau Melissa & Associates
7700 University
Des Moines IA, 50325
(515) 277-8308
Specialty: G
Employment Agency/Recruiter

Doug Ryan CPC, Pres
Bryant Bureau
2435 Kimberly Road #110 North
Bettendorf, IA 52722
(800) 873-4411
(319) 355-3635 FAX
Specialty: S
Employment Agency/Recruiter

Office Manager
C S I Employment & Recruiting
319 N Main St
Burlington, IA 52601
(319) 753-0223
Specialty: G
Employment Agency/Recruiter

Office Manager
Cafe Beaudelaire
2504 Lincoln Way
Ames, IA 50010
(515) 292-7429
Specialty: G
Employment Agency/Recruiter

Office Manager
Cambridge & Assocs Inc
400 S Clinton St Ste 208
Iowa City, IA 52240
(319) 354-8281
Specialty: G
Employment Agency/Recruiter

Office Manager
Cambridge Permanent Employment
Cedar River Tower
1st Avenue & 1st St NE
Cedar Rapids, IA 52401-1134
(712) 366-7771
Specialty: B,C,E,F,H,O,S
Employment Agency/Recruiter

Office Manager
Cambridge Temp Positions
Cedar River Tower # 7
Cedar Rapids, IA 52401
(319) 362-9555
Specialty: G
Employment Agency/Recruiter

Office Manager
Career Finders
7517 Douglas Avenue Ste 7
Urbandale, IA 50322
(712) 278-9467
(712) 278-9470 FAX
Specialty: O,S,Management
Employment Agency/Recruiter

Office Manager
Careers Inc
805 W 35th St
Davenport, IA 52801
(319) 386-1986
Specialty: G
Employment Agency/Recruiter

Office Manager
Career Resources
820 1st Street
West Des Moines, IA 50265
(515) 255-4923
Specialty: G
Personnel Consultant/Recruiter

Office Manager
Careers Unlimited
1309 1st Ave S
Fort Dodge, IA 50501
(515) 573-4414
Specialty: G
Employment Agency/Recruiter

Office Manager
Career Search Associates
Regency West 5
4500 Westown Pkwy Ste 115
Des Moines, IA 50266
(515) 224-2183
Specialty: O
Employment Agency/Recruiter

Office Manager
Chenhall Personnel Services
203 Kahl Bldg
Davenport, IA 52801
(319) 324-2166
Specialty: G
Employment Agency/Recruiter

Office Manager
CareerNet
2120 Grand Avenue
Des Moines, IA 50312
(515) 244-3902
Specialty: G
Employment Agency/Recruiter

Office Manager
City & National Employment
221 E 4th St
Waterloo, IA 50703
(319) 232-6641
Specialty: G
Employment Agency/Recruiter

Employment Agencies/Recruiters

Office Manager
Compu-Search
Alpine Centre South Penthouse
Bettendorf, IA 52722
(319) 359-3503
Specialty: C
Employment Agency/Recruiter

Office Manager
Corporate Suite Ltd
507 Merle Hay Tower
Des Moines, IA 50310
(515) 278-2744
Specialty: G
Employment Agency/Recruiter

Office Manager
Dan Frommelt Personnel
1702 Woodland Ave
Des Moines, IA 50309
(515) 283-0925
Specialty: G
Employment Agency/Recruiter

Office Manager
Dee Springer Personnel
2435 Kimberly Rd
Bettendorf, IA 52722
(319) 355-0241
Specialty: G
Employment Agency/Recruiter

Office Manager
Deskins Technology
332 Highley Building
118 3rd Avenue SE
Cedar Rapids, IA 52401
(515) 363-8661
Specialty: C
Employment Agency/Recruiter

Office Manager
DP Search
1200 Valley West Dr Ste 206-6
West Des Moines, IA 50266
(515) 223-8910
Specialty: C
Employment Agency/Recruiter

Office Manager
Employee Resources Inc
2774 University Ave
Dubuque, IA 52001
(319) 557-1443
Specialty: G
Employment Agency/Recruiter

Office Manager
Employment Consultants
204 Collins Rd NE Suite 203
Cedar Rapids, IA 52402
(319) 377-7344
Specialty: G
Employment Agency/Recruiter

Office Manager
Employment Services Centers
1315 Jersey Ridge Rd
Davenport, IA 52803
(319) 322-0515
Specialty: G
Employment Agency/Recruiter

Office Manager
Excel Employment Services
625 Court Street
Sioux City, IA 51101
(712) 252-3871
Specialty: G
Employment Agency/Recruiter

Office Manager
Execu Med Recruiters
221 E 4 Street
Waterloo, IA 50703
(319) 232-6641
Specialty: H
Employment Agency/Recruiter

Office Manager
Executive Resources Ltd
3716 Ingersoll Ave Ste B
Des Moines, IA 50312
(515) 287-6880
Specialty: G
Employment Agency/Recruiter

Office Manager
Expertise Personnel Inc
1854 Fuller Road
West Des Moines, IA 50265
(515) 225-7125
Specialty: G
Employment Agency/Recruiter

Richard or Jennifer Langowski, Owners
Express Personnel Services
1415 4th Street SW
Mason City, IA 50401
(515) 423-5613
(515) 423-0757 FAX
Specialty: G
Employment Agency/Recruiter

Office Manager
Express Services Temporary
4807 University Ave
Cedar Falls, IA 50613
(319) 277-6603
Specialty: G
Employment Agency/Recruiter

Office Manager
Gadbury Temporary Employment
809 Central Av Suite 430
Fort Dodge, IA 50501
(515) 955-8885
Specialty: G
Employment Agency/Recruiter

Employment Agencies/Recruiters

Office Manager
Hamilton Thomas
400 Locust St Suite 690
Des Moines, IA 50309
(515) 282-0221
Specialty: G
Employment Agency/Recruiter

Office Manager
Help Inc
1227 S Main
Council Bluff, IA 51503
(319) 322-2135
Specialty: G
Employment Agency/Recruiter

Office Manager
Human Resource Group
600 5th Avenue Plaza
Des Moines, IA 50309
(515) 243-8855
Specialty: G
Employment Agency/Recruiter

Office Manager
IA Comprehensive Human Service Inc
301 S 11th Ave W
Newton, IA 50208
(515) 791-9308
Specialty: G
Employment Agency/Recruiter

Office Manager
Insight Companies
601 Locust Street
Des Moines, IA 50309
(515) 245-3793
Specialty: G
Personnel Consultant/Recruiter

Office Manager
Interim Personnel
1490 NW 86 Street
Clive, IA 50325
(515) 223-5532
Specialty: G
Employment Agency/Recruiter

Office Manager
Interstate Personnel Service
P O Box 1167
North Sioux City, IA 51102
(712) 232-9119
Specialty: G
Personnel Consultant/Recruiter

Office Manager
Iowa Job Service
51 W Washington Ave
Fairfield, IA 52556
(515) 472-5466
Specialty: G
Employment Agency/Recruiter

Office Manager
**Job Corps Applications
& Placement**
902 W Kimberly Rd
Davenport, IA 52806
(319) 386-2120
Specialty: G
Employment Agency/Recruiter

Office Manager
Job Service of Iowa
2700 1st Ave S
Fort Dodge, IA 50501
(515) 576-0741
Specialty: G
Employment Agency/Recruiter

Office Manager
**Job Market LTD Personnel
Services**
412 Loras Blvd
Dubuque, IA 52001
(319) 556-1714
Specialty: G
Employment Agency/Recruiter

Office Manager
Job Service of Iowa
354 Public Sq
Greenfield, IA 50849
(515) 743-2433
Specialty: G
Employment Agency/Recruiter

Office Manager
Job Service of Iowa
215 N Elm St
Creston, IA 50801
(515) 782-2119
Specialty: G
Employment Agency/Recruiter

Office Manager
Job Service of Iowa
208 West St
Grinnell, IA 50112
(515) 236-4732
Specialty: G
Employment Agency/Recruiter

Office Manager
Job Service of Iowa
902 W Kimberly Rd
Davenport, IA 52806
(319) 386-4770
Specialty: G
Employment Agency/Recruiter

Office Manager
Job Service of Iowa
123 E Jefferson St
Osceola, IA 50213
(515) 342-4955
Specialty: G
Employment Agency/Recruiter

Employment Agencies/Recruiters 71

Office Manager
Job Service of Iowa
128 3rd St NW
Sioux Center, IA 51250
(712) 722-4813
Specialty: G
Employment Agency/Recruiter

Office Manager
Job Training Area VII
101 N Locust St Ste 213
New Hampton, IA 50659
(515) 394-4732
Specialty: G
Employment Agency/Recruiter

Office Manager
Job Training Program
315 5 Avenue S
Clinton, IA 52732
(319) 243-9060
Specialty: G
Employment Agency/Recruiter

Office Manager
JTPA Area 8
799 Main Street
Dubuque, IA 52001
(319) 556-4166
Specialty: G
Employment Agency/Recruiter

Office Manager
Key Employment Services
1001 Office Park Rd Ste 320
West Des Moines, IA 50265
(515) 224-0446
Specialty: B,C,E,F,I,
Retail,Industrial,Management
Employment Agency/Recruiter

Office Manager
Koster & Kompany
7799 University Avenue Ste A
Des Moines, IA 50325
(712) 255-4311
Specialty: S
Employment Agency/Recruiter

Mitchell Smith, Office Manager
Lee Smith & Associates
7177 Hickman Road Ste 11
Des Moines, IA 50322
(515) 270-2791
(515) 270-8708 FAX
Specialty: H,S
Employment Agency/Recruiter

Office Manager
Management Recruiters
2435 Kimberly Rd
Bettendorf, IA 52722
(319) 359-3503
Specialty: G
Employment Agency/Recruiter

Office Manager
Management Recruiters
1009 Hwy 6 W Ste 7
Coralville, IA 52241
(319) 354-4320
Specialty: G
Employment Agency/Recruiter

Office Manager
Management Recruiters
520 S Pierce Ave Ste 202
Mason City, IA 50401
(515) 424-1680
Specialty: G
Employment Agency/Recruiter

Office Manager
**Management Recruiters
of Des Moines**
7400 University Avenue
Clive, IA 50325
(515) 255-1242
Specialty: G
Employment Agency/Recruiter

Office Manager
Management Resource Group
400 Main St
Davenport, IA 52801
(319) 323-3333
Specialty: G
Employment Agency/Recruiter

Office Manager
Mangement Recruiters
Ste 400 Brenton Bank Bldg
150 First Avenue NE
Cedar Rapids, IA 52401
(712) 366-8441
Specialty: E,H,O,S
Employment Agency/Recruiter

Office Manager
McGladrey Search Group
400 Locust St Ste 690
Des Moines, IA 50309
(515) 282-0221
Specialty: B,C,E,F,H,I,O,P,S
Employment Agency/Recruiter

Office Manager
McKirchy & Co Inc
2535 Tech Dr Ste 104
Bettendorf, IA 52722
(319) 332-8888
Specialty: G
Employment Agency/Recruiter

Office Manager
Medical Personnel Pool of Iowa
1490 NW 86th St
Des Moines, IA 50325
(515) 223-5500
Specialty: H
Employment Agency/Recruiter

montgomery®

Employment Agencies/Recruiters 73

Office Manager
Metro Temp
5906 SW 9 Street
Des Moines, IA 50315
(515) 285-8367
Specialty: G
Employment Agency/Recruiter

Office Manager
Mid American Search
4401 Weston Pkwy Ste 226
West Des Moines, IA 50266
(515) 225-1942
Specialty: I
Employment Agency/Recruiter

Connie Whitcomb, Sys Spc
Mid-States Technical
Staffing Services Inc
2435 Kimberly Rd Ste 225 S
Bettendorf, IA 52722-3505
(319) 359-7042
(319) 359-6331 FAX
Specialty: E
Employment Agency/Recruiter

Office Manager
Midtown Personnel
300 Metropolitan Federal
Bank Bldg
Council Bluffs, IA 51503
(712) 328-3153
Specialty: F,H,I,L,O,
S,T,Electronics, Retail
Employment Agency/Recruiter

Office Manager
Murphy Employment Service
411 1st Ave SE Ste 202
Cedar Rapids, IA 52401
(712) 364-6195
Specialty: G
Employment Agency/Recruiter

Office Manager
National Employment
Wire Service
2010 S Ankeny Blvd
Ankeny, IA 50021
(515) 964-6718
Specialty: G
Employment Agency/Recruiter

Office Manager
National Healthcare
Placement Assoc
501 Sycamore Bldg
Waterloo, IA 50703
(319) 233-3202
Specialty: H
Employment Agency/Recruiter

Office Manager
New Focus Inc
102 W Washington
Centerville, IA 52544
(515) 437-1722
Specialty: G
Employment Agency/Recruiter

Office Manager
Oakstone Consulting
1315 Jersey Ridge Rd Suite 1
Davenport, IA 52803
(319) 322-0515
Specialty: G
Employment Agency/Recruiter

Office Manager
Off-Duty Police Services
3017 Indianola Avenue
Des Moines, IA 50315
(515) 280-3521
Specialty: G
Personnel Consultant/Recruiter

Office Manager
Office Mates 5
S Alpine Centre Penthouse
Bettendorf, IA 52722
(319) 359-1681
Specialty: O
Employment Agency/Recruiter

Office Manager
Office Mates 5
150 1st Av NE Ste 400
Cedar Rapids, IA 52401
(319) 366-8444
Specialty: O
Employment Agency/Recruiter

Office Manager
Personnel Incorporated
516 Equitable Building
Des Moines, IA 50309
(515) 243-7687
Specialty: G
Personnel Consultant/Recruiter

Office Manager
Personnel Pool Temporary Svcs
860 2 Avenue SE
Cedar Rapids, IA 52403
(319) 364-8352
Specialty: G
Employment Agency/Recruiter

Office Manager
Personnel Professionals
2205 Camanche Avenue
Clinton, IA 52732
(319) 242-1078
Specialty: G
Employment Agency/Recruiter

Office Manager
Pipeline Placement Ltd
River Hills Mall
Iowa Falls, IA 50126
(515) 648-2539
Specialty: G
Employment Agency/Recruiter

Employment Agencies/Recruiters 75

Office Manager
Pratt Younglove
715 Francis Building
505 Fifth Street
Sioux City, IA 51101
(712) 255-7961
Specialty: G
Employment Agency/Recruiter

Office Manager
Preferred Personnel
2940 Des Moines St
Des Moines, IA 50317
(515) 262-9061
Specialty: G
Employment Agency/Recruiter

Office Manager
Pro-Tech of Des Moines Ltd
4900 University Avenue
Des Moines, IA 50311
(515) 255-0909
Specialty: O,Technical
Employment Agency/Recruiter

Office Manager
Professional Placement
503 Iowa Ave
Muscatine, IA 52761
(319) 263-6589
Specialty: G
Employment Agency/Recruiter

Office Manager
Project Assist
1631 Isett Ave
Muscatine, IA 52761
(319) 264-3346
Specialty: G
Employment Agency/Recruiter

Office Manager
Proteus Employment
659 12th St
Marion, IA 52302
(319) 377-3039
Specialty: G
Employment Agency/Recruiter

Office Manager
Proteus Employment Opportunities Inc
2307 5th Ave S
Fort Dodge, IA 50501
(515) 573-8225
Specialty: G
Employment Agency/Recruiter

Office Manager
Quality Recruiters Inc
Warden Plz Ste M27
Fort Dodge, IA 50501
(515) 573-2400
Specialty: G
Employment Agency/Recruiter

Mike Foster, Pres
R Michael's & Associates Inc
2424 40th Avenue
Moline, IL 61265
(309) 762-2804
(309) 762-2844 FAX
Specialty: E,M,P,R,S
Employment Agency/Recruiter

Office Manager
Rose Leonetti & Associates Inc
600 Fifth Avenue Plaza
Des Moines, IA 50309
(515) 282-3232
Specialty: G
Employment Agency/Recruiter

Office Manager
Resource Placement Group III
221 E 4th Street
Waterloo, IA 50703
(319) 232-6641
Specialty: G
Employment Agency/Recruiter

Office Manager
Roth Young Personnel Services
1025 Ashworth Road Ste 532
West Des Moines, IA 50265
(515) 222-0675
Specialty: H,T,Retail,Food & Drug, Supermarket
Employment Agency/Recruiter

Office Manager
Rhodes-Shanley & Associates
600 5 Av Plaza
Des Moines, IA 50309
(515) 245-2000
Specialty: G
Personnel Consultant/Recruiter

Steve Salem, Pres
Rudy Salem Employment Agency
300 Pioneer Bank Building
P O Box 3124
Sioux City, IA 51102
(712) 277-4204
(712) 277-1512 FAX
Specialty: G
Employment Agency/Recruiter

Office Manager
Robert Half International
317 6th Ave Ste 700
Des Moines, IA 50309
(515) 244-4414
Specialty: B,C,F
Employment Agency/Recruiter

Office Manager
S E A R C H 21
206 NE 8th St
Ankeny, IA 50021
(515) 964-2165
Specialty: G
Employment Agency/Recruiter

Office Manager
Sac Co Outreach Center
622 Park Ave
Sac City, IA 50583
(712) 662-3236
Specialty: G
Employment Agency/Recruiter

Office Manager
Sales Consultants of Cedar Rapids
200 1 Ave NE Ste 203
Cedar Rapids, IA 52401
(712) 365-8900
Specialty: S
Employment Agency/Recruiter

Office Manager
Sales Resources
3716 Ingersoll Avenue
Des Moines, IA 50312
(515) 287-6880
Specialty: S
Employment Agency/Recruiter

Office Manager
Sales Search
4500 Westown Pky Ste 115
West Des Moines, IA 50265
(515) 224-2180
Specialty: S
Employment Agency/Recruiter

Office Manager
Snelling & Snelling
2201 5th Avenue
Moline, IL 61265
(309) 797-1101
Specialty: G
Employment Agency/Recruiter

Office Manager
Snelling Personnel Services
1452 29 Street
West Des Moines, IA 50266
(515) 223-8888
Specialty: G
Employment Agency/Recruiter

Office Manager
Spectrum Personnel Ltd
114 Mulberry Ave
Muscatine, IA 52761
(319) 263-0337
Specialty: G
Employment Agency/Recruiter

Office Manager
Spence Ewing & Associates
218 6 Ave Ste 420
Des Moines, IA 50309
(515) 283-2473
Specialty: G
Employment Agency/Recruiter

Paul Olsen, Gen Manager
Staff Associates/Staff Temps
974 73rd Street Ste 42
Des Moines, IA 50312-1026
(515) 224-1569
(515) 224-0908 FAX
Specialty: G,O,Management Trainees
Employment Agency/Recruiter

Office Manager
The Williamson Group Inc
Regency West 5
4500 Westown Pkwy Ste 115
Des Moines, IA 50266
(515) 224-2180
Specialty: B,C,F,H,I,Retail, Industrial
Employment Agency/Recruiter

Office Manager
Strategicare Personnel Services
1452 29 St Ste 216
West Des Moines, IA 50266
(515) 224-5890
Specialty: G
Employment Agency/Recruiter

Office Manager
Tucker Personnel Consultants
1728 34 St NE
Cedar Rapids, IA 52402
(319) 362-2936
Specialty: G
Employment Agency/Recruiter

Office Manager
Tempro Services Inc
612 Valley View Dr
Moline, IL 61265
(309) 797-8367
Specialty: G
Employment Agency/Recruiter

Office Manager
United Personnel Inc
1921 5th Avenue
Moline, IL 61265
(309) 762-6891
Specialty: G
Employment Agency/Recruiter

Office Manager
The Future Employment Service
440 Fischer Bldg
Dubuque, IA 52001
(319) 556-3040
Specialty: G
Employment Agency/Recruiter

Office Manager
Viall Nate & Associates
P O Box 12238
Des Moines, IA 50312
(515) 274-1729
Specialty: G
Employment Agency/Recruiter

Employment Agencies/Recruiters

Office Manager
Weinstein S E Company
1830 2nd Avenue
Rock Island, IL 61201
(309) 794-1992
Specialty: G
Personnel Consultant/Recruiter

Office Manager
Western Temporary Svcs
4089 21st Ave SW Ste 214
Cedar Rapids, IA 52404
(319) 390-3737
Specialty: G
Employment Agency/Recruiter

Office Manager
Western Temporary Svcs
715 Frances Building
Sioux City, IA 51101
(712) 277-2580
Specialty: G
Employment Agency/Recruiter

Office Manager
Williams & Company
814 Pierce St
Sioux City, IA 51101
(712) 252-4041
Specialty: G
Personnel Consultant/Recruiter

Office Manager
X-Pertise Personnel Inc
1854 Fuller Road
West Des Moines, IA 50265
(515) 225-7125
Specialty: G
Employment Agency/Recruiter

JOB SEEKERS SURVIVAL HINTS

Make effective use of your time -- "Let Your Fingers Do the Walking". Use the telephone to maximize your time when contacting companies to arrange interviews.

In a given day it is possible to contact over fifty companies by phone to quickly determine if they have an opening and to arrange for a personal interview.

Identify and list potential companies to be called. When calling, ask for the name of the department head sought and then request to be connected with that person. When the department head comes on the line, address them by name and introduce yourself along with your background.

Avoid asking "Do you have any positions open?", the answer is almost always "No". Instead use this opportunity to ask for an interview to discuss possible job openings.

If the employer agrees to meet, schedule the interview as soon as possible. Since you want to schedule your interviews in the afternoon suggest that time slot.

If there is absolutely no possibility of meeting with them, then ask them about any other companies that they could recommend calling.

Employment Agencies/Recruiters - Kansas

The following pages contain the specialty cross-reference listings to an alphabetical list of active employment agencies/recruiters located in Kansas.

The alphabetical listing is immediately after the cross-reference list.

INDEX CROSS REFERENCE BY SPECIALTY

Specialty: A
(Advertising)

Nationwide Advertising Svc

Specialty: B
(Banking)

Accounttemps
Career Advancement
Financial Careers
Hoag Pointer Personnel

Specialty: C
(Computers & Data Processing)

Accounttemps
Check-Mate Careers of Wichita
DP Career Associates
Dunhill of Wichita Inc
Dunhill Personnel
Effective Search
Human Resources Group
Kennison & Associates
Morgan Hunter Corp
Source EDP
Staffing Solutions Inc
YWCA Career Assistance
    Network

Specialty: E
(Engineering)

Advanced Careers
Austin Nichols Technical Search
Career Advancement
Dunhill of Wichita Inc
Dunhill Personnel
Effective Search
Engineering Associates
Kennison & Associates
Management Recruiters
    of Topeka Inc

Specialty: F
(Finance & Accounting)

Accounttemps
Advanced Careers
Bossler-Hix Personnel
Career Advancement
Dunhill Personnel
Hoag Pointer Personnel
Human Resources Group
Management Recruiters
    of Topeka Inc
Morgan Hunter Corp
Office Mates 5
Staffing Solutions Inc

Specialty: G
(General Applications)

Able Employment Inc
Adia Personnel Svc
Adia The Employment People
Alline Personnel Svc

Employment Agencies/Recruiters

Amega Inc
Arthur Lee & Assoc
Best Personnel Svc
Bossler/Brown
Bossler-Hix Personnel
Brack Hunter Corp
Brin Company
Business Specialists
Chapple Group Inc The
Colby Employment & Training
Commercial Vending
CompuSearch
Cooper & Associates
Dunhill Professional Search
Eleventh Hour Personnel
Employ America Of KC Inc
Express Services
George Waterman Executive
Gerson Personnel Svc
Green Myron & Assoc Inc
Hensler & Assoc
Int'l Technical Services
Interim Personnel of Kansas
J T Nelson & Assoc
Jensen Personnel Svc Co
Job Service Ctr
JTPA
Kaplan & Assoc
Ketch Employment Services
Kimble Keith & Assocs Inc
L S I Corp
Malcolm Miller Inc
Management Recruiters
Management Recruiters Wanamaker
Martin Kate & Associates
Midwest Search Group
Mitchell & Assoc
Morse Recruiting
Mueller Busby Personnel
National Personnel Assoc
Nichols Personnel Inc
Northern Cross
Office Mates 5
PARR & Assoc
Patti Bossert
Personametrics Inc
Personnel Services Inc
Personnel Solutions Inc
Premiere Staffing
Private Industry Council
Professional Search
Robert Half
Rollheiser & Assoc
Scully & Associates Inc
Senior Employment Ctr
Senior Employment Program
SER Corp Jobs For Progress
Signature Staffing Inc
Source Finance
Starkey Developmental Ctr Inc
Stoneburner Associates
Synstrata Corp Inc
The Chapple Group Inc
TOP Personnel Services
Topeka Youth Project
Wayne-Keith-Simpson Intl
White & Assoc
Wichita Services Inc
William Lawrence & Assoc
Work Options
Wright Business School
WSA Corp
Wyatt & Associates Inc
YWCA Career Assistance Network

YWCA Employment & Resource Network-Earn

Specialty: H
(Healthcare)

Communi-Care/Pro-Rehab
Health Search Inc
Hoag Pointer Personnel
Management Recruiters of Topeka Inc
Med Resources
Office Mates 5
Preferred Medical Placement

Specialty: I
(Insurance)

Management Recruiters of Topeka Inc
Morgan Hunter Corp

Specialty: L
(Legal)

Hoag Pointer Personnel
Legal Personnel
Legal Search Assoc
Office Mates 5
Professional Employment Services Inc

Specialty: M
(Manufacturing)

Advanced Careers
Career Advancement
Dunhill of Wichita Inc
Management Recruiters of Topeka Inc
YWCA Career Assistance Network

Specialty: O
(Office Administration)

Bar Association Legal Placement
Dunhill Personnel
Hoag Pointer Personnel
Morgan Hunter Corp
Office Mates 5
Professional Employment Services Inc
Staffing Solutions Inc

Specialty: P
(Personnel & Human Resources)

Advanced Careers
Career Advancement
Human Resources Group

Specialty: S
(Sales & Marketing)

Advanced Careers
Dunhill of Wichita Inc
Dunhill Personnel
Hoag Pointer Personnel

Management Recruiters
   of Topeka Inc
Professional Employment
   Services Inc
Sales Consultants
Staffing Solutions Inc

Professional Employment
   Services Inc

OTHER SPECIFIC SPECIALTIES:

Specialty: Environmental

Austin Nichols Technical Search

Specialty: Food Service

Professional Employment
   Services Inc

Specialty: Nannies

Nanny Placement Markham

Specialty: Professional

Professional Employment
   Services Inc

Specialty: Technical

Austin Nichols Technical Search
Effective Search

Office Manager
Able Employment Inc
8819 Long St
Shawnee Mission, KS 66215
(913) 894-1200
Specialty: G
Employment Agency/Recruiter

Mary Jo Smith, Branch Manager
Accounttemps
1 Metropolitan Square Ste 2130
St Louis, MO 63102
(314) 621-8367
(314) 621-4967 FAX
Specialty: B,C,F,
Temporary Placement
Employment Agency/Recruiter

Office Manager
Adia Personnel Svc
100 E 9th St
Lawrence, KS 66044
(913) 842-1515
Specialty: G
Employment Agency/Recruiter

Office Manager
Adia Personnel Svc
8300 College Blvd
Shawnee Mission, KS 66210
(913) 451-8070
Specialty: G
Employment Agency/Recruiter

Office Manager
Adia The Employment People
2804 E Central
Wichita, KS 67214
(316) 686-3222
Specialty: G
Employment Agency/Recruiter

Hal Willis CPC, VP
Advanced Careers
6528 Raytown Road Ste I
Kansas City, MO 64133
(816) 358-3553
(816) 358-3566 FAX
Specialty: E,F,M,P,S
Employment Agency/Recruiter

Office Manager
Alline Personnel Svc
1601 Longhorn Dr
Garden City, KS 67846
(316) 275-6364
Specialty: G
Employment Agency/Recruiter

Office Manager
Amega Inc
4759 Rainbow Blvd
Kansas City, KS 66103
(913) 722-6225
Specialty: G
Employment Agency/Recruiter

Employment Agencies/Recruiters

Office Manager
Arthur Lee & Assoc
11111 Nall Ave
Shawnee Mission, KS 66211
(913) 491-0800
Specialty: G
Employment Agency/Recruiter

Office Manager
Bossler/Brown
1035 SW Topeka Avenue
Topeka, KS 66612
(913) 234-5626
Specialty: G
Employment Agency/Recruiter

Dave McDowell
Austin Nichols Technical Search
1100 Main St Ste 1670
Kansas City, MO 64105
(816) 471-5575
Specialty: E,Environmental,
Technical
Employment Agency/Recruiter

Ann Duwe, Mgr
Bossler-Hix Personnel
11015 Metcalf Ave
Overland Park, KS 66210
(913) 491-0944
Specialty: F
Employment Agency/Recruiter

Office Manager
Bar Association Legal Placement
301 N Main Street
Wichita, KS 67202
(316) 263-2469
Specialty: O(Support Staff For
Attorneys)
Employment Agency/Recruiter

Office Manager
Bossler-Hix Personnel
6405 Metcalf Ave
Shawnee Mission, KS 66202
(913) 384-6161
Specialty: G
Employment Agency/Recruiter

Office Manager
Best Personnel Svc
14201 S Mur Len Rd Ste 106
Olathe, KS 66062
(913) 829-5848
Specialty: G
Employment Agency/Recruiter

Office Manager
Brack Hunter Corp
6333 Long St
Shawnee Mission, KS 66216
(913) 631-1040
Specialty: G
Employment Agency/Recruiter

Office Manager
Brin Company
3500 N Rock Rd
Wichita, KS 67226
(316) 636-2752
Specialty: G
Employment Agency/Recruiter

Office Manager
Check-Mate Careers of Wichita
P O Box 21017
Wichita, KS 67208
(316) 744-3777
Specialty: C
Employment Agency/Recruiter

Office Manager
Business Specialists
105 S Broadway Street
Wichita, KS 67202
(316) 267-7375
Specialty: G
Employment Agency/Recruiter

Office Manager
Colby Employment & Training
485 N Chick Ave
Colby, KS 67701
(913) 462-6862
Specialty: G
Employment Agency/Recruiter

Tony Stutey, Pres
Career Advancement
1525 W 29th St N
Wichita, KS 67204
(316) 838-2626
Specialty: B,E,F,M,P
Contingency/Retainer Recruiter

Office Manager
Commercial Vending
113 N Handley St
Wichita, KS 67203
(316) 262-2131
Specialty: G
Employment Agency/Recruiter

Office Manager
Chapple Group Inc The
113 N Handley St
Wichita, KS 67203
(316) 262-2131
Specialty: G
Employment Agency/Recruiter

Rebecca Henderson, Recruiter
Communi-Care/Pro-Rehab
1709 E 21st Terrrace
Lawrence, KS 66046
(913) 865-1588
Specialty: H
Recruiter

Employment Agencies/Recruiters

Office Manager
CompuSearch
9401 Indian Creek Pkwy
Overland Park, KS 66210
(913) 661-9400
Specialty: G
Employment Agency/Recruiter

Office Manager
Cooper & Associates
417 Commercial Street
Emporia, KS 66810
(316) 343-7232
Specialty: G
Employment Agency/Recruiter

Ron Maupin, Pres
DP Career Associates
6405 Metcalf Ste 502
Overland Park, KS 66202
(913) 236-8288
(913) 236-9748 FAX
Specialty: C
Employment Agency

Office Manager
Dunhill of Wichita Inc
425 N Broadway Street
Wichita, KS 67202
(316) 265-9541
Specialty: C,E,M,S
Employment Agency/Recruiter

Office Manager
Dunhill Personnel
150 SW 33rd Street
Topeka, KS 66611
(913) 267-2773
Specialty: C,E,F,O,S
Employment Agency/Recruiter

Office Manager
Dunhill Professional Search
7101 College Blvd Ste 120
Shawnee Mission, KS 66210
(913) 451-8333
Specialty: G
Employment Agency/Recruiter

Office Manager
Effective Search
301 N Main
Wichita, KS 67202
(316) 267-9180
Specialty: C,E,Technical
Employment Agency/Recruiter

Linda Long
Eleventh Hour Personnel
11720 W 95th St Ste G7
Overland Park, KS 66214
(913) 492-8431
Specialty: G
Employment Agency/Recruiter

Office Manager
Employ America Of KC Inc
6950 Squibb Rd
Shawnee Mission, KS 66202
(913) 831-0300
Specialty: G
Employment Agency/Recruiter

Office Manager
Engineering Associates
8500 College Blvd
Shawnee Mission, KS 66210
(913) 451-6130
Specialty: E
Employment Agency/Recruiter

Office Manager
Express Services
3129 SW Huntoon Street
Topeka, KS 66604
(913) 232-6611
Specialty: G
Employment Agency/Recruiter

Jennifer Bryant, Mgr
Financial Careers
6405 Metcalf Ave Ste 418
Overland Park, KS 66202
(913) 262-8635
(913) 262-8634 FAX
Specialty: B
Employment Agency/Recruiter

Office Manager
George Waterman Executive
11879 W 112th St
Shawnee Mission, KS 66210
(913) 451-4448
Specialty: G
Employment Agency/Recruiter

Office Manager
Gerson Personnel Svc
6950 Squibb Rd Ste 404
Shawnee Mission, KS 66202
(913) 262-7254
Specialty: G
Employment Agency/Recruiter

Office Manager
Green Myron & Assoc Inc
412 Miami Ave
Kansas City, KS 66202
(913) 371-6991
Specialty: G
Employment Agency/Recruiter

Office Manager
Health Search Inc
1330 E 1st Street N
Wichita, KS 67214
(316) 265-1210
Specialty: H
Employment Agency/Recruiter

Employment Agencies/Recruiters

Office Manager
Hensler & Assoc
9300 W 110th St
Shawnee Mission, KS 66210
(913) 451-9460
Specialty: G
Employment Agency/Recruiter

Office Manager
Hoag Pointer Personnel
3601 SW 29th St Ste 131
SW Plaza Building
Topeka, KS 66614
(913) 273-2833
Specialty: B,F,H,L,O,S
Employment Agency/Recruiter

Mike Rivera, Sr Recruiter
Human Resources Group
4707 College Blvd Ste 213
Leawood, KS 66211
(913) 491-6609
(800) 484-8011
(913) 345-0580
Specialty: C,E,P
Employment Agency/Recruiter

Office Manager
Int'l Technical Services
214 S Rock Rd
Wichita, KS 67207
(316) 686-8589
Specialty: G
Employment Agency/Recruiter

Maxine Martin, Branch Mgr
Interim Personnel of Kansas
1601 W 23rd St Ste 106
Lawrence, KS 66046
(913) 832-1290
(913) 832-1292 FAX
Specialty: G
Employment Agency/Recruiter

Office Manager
J T Nelson & Assoc
7700 W 63rd St Ste 5
Kansas City, KS 66102
(913) 236-9433
Specialty: G
Employment Agency/Recruiter

Office Manager
Jensen Personnel Svc Co
10310 State Line
Kansas City, KS 66103
(913) 341-1944
Specialty: G
Employment Agency/Recruiter

Office Manager
Job Service Ctr
1102 Elm St
Coffeyville, KS 67337
(316) 251-1800
Specialty: G
Employment Agency/Recruiter

Office Manager
JTPA
512 Market St
Emporia, KS 66801
(316) 343-6542
Specialty: G
Employment Agency/Recruiter

Office Manager
Kaplan & Assoc
10540 Marty St
Shawnee Mission, KS 66212
(913) 341-3900
Specialty: G
Employment Agency/Recruiter

Gary F Fawkes CPC
Kennison & Associates
4200 Pennsylvania Ave Ste 210
Kansas City, MO 64111
(816) 753-4401
Specialty: C,E
Employment Agency/Recruiter

Office Manager
Ketch Employment Services
1020 E Waterman St
Wichita, KS 67211
(316) 269-7745
Specialty: G
Employment Agency/Recruiter

Office Manager
Ketch Employment Svcs
1901 Delaware St
Lawrence, KS 66046
(913) 832-3700
Specialty: G
Employment Agency/Recruiter

Office Manager
Kimble Keith & Assocs Inc
12351 W 96th Terr
Shawnee Mission, KS 66215
(913) 599-2344
Specialty: G
Employment Agency/Recruiter

Office Manager
L S I Corp
519 S Broadway
Wichita, KS 67202
(316) 262-0162
Specialty: G
Employment Agency/Recruiter

Office Manager
Legal Personnel
6803 W 64th St
Shawnee Mission, KS 66202
(913) 677-0510
Specialty: L
Employment Agency/Recruiter

Employment Agencies/Recruiters 93

Office Manager
Legal Search Assoc
6701 W 64th St Ste 304
Shawnee Mission, KS 66202
(913) 722-3500
Specialty: L
Employment Agency/Recruiter

Office Manager
Malcolm Miller Inc
11900 College Blvd
Shawnee Mission, KS 66210
(913) 469-0000
Specialty: G
Employment Agency/Recruiter

Office Manager
Management Recruiters
2500 W 6th
Lawrence, KS 66049
(913) 841-8777
Specialty: G
Employment Agency/Recruiter

Office Manager
Management Recruiters
9401 Indian Creek Pkwy
Overland Park, KS 66210
(913) 661-9300
Specialty: G
Employment Agency/Recruiter

Office Manager
Management Recruiters
8441 E 32nd St N
Wichita, KS 67226
(316) 634-1971
Specialty: G
Employment Agency/Recruiter

Office Manager
Management Recruiters
of Topeka Inc
3400 SW Van Buren Street
Topeka, KS 66611
(913) 267-5430
Specialty: E,F,H,I,M,S
Employment Agency/Recruiter

Office Manager
Management Recruiters
-Wanamaker
2900 SW Wanamaker Drive
Topeka, KS 66614
(913) 273-1221
Specialty: G
Employment Agency/Recruiter

Office Manager
Martin Kate & Associates
400 N Woodlawn St
Wichita, KS 67208
(316) 652-7400
Specialty: G
Employment Agency/Recruiter

Office Manager
Med Resources
8105 W 99th St
Shawnee Mission, KS 66212
(913) 648-6064
Specialty: H
Employment Agency/Recruiter

Office Manager
Midwest Search Group
9344 Mission Rd
Shawnee Mission, KS 66206
(913) 381-7711
Specialty: G
Employment Agency/Recruiter

Office Manager
Mitchell & Assoc
6100 Martway St
Shawnee Mission, KS 66202
(913) 677-2724
Specialty: G
Employment Agency/Recruiter

Jerry Hellebusch, Owner
Morgan Hunter Corp
6800 College Blvd Ste 550
Overland Park, KS 66211
(913) 491-3434
Specialty: C,F,I,O
Employment Agency/Recruiter

Office Manager
Morse Recruiting
4550 W 109th St
Shawnee Mission, KS 66211
(913) 491-3344
Specialty: G
Employment Agency/Recruiter

Office Manager
Mueller Busby Personnel
5020 SW 28th Street
Topeka, KS 66614
(913) 273-3991
Specialty: G
Employment Agency/Recruiter

Office Manager
Nanny Placement Markham
14700 W Kellogg
Wichita, KS 67235
(316) 722-5660
Specialty: Nannies
Employment Agency/Recruiter

Office Manager
National Personnel Assoc
5104 Foxridge Dr
Shawnee Mission, KS 66202
(913) 384-3056
Specialty: G
Employment Agency/Recruiter

Employment Agencies/Recruiters

Office Manager
Nationwide Advertising Svc
250 N Rock Rd
Wichita, KS 67206
(316) 682-4576
Specialty: A
Employment Agency/Recruiter

Ann Doerflinger, Pres
Nichols Personnel Inc
9201 Ward Parkway Ste 306
Kansas City, MO 64114
(816) 444-5910
(816) 444-5947 FAX
Specialty: G
Employment Agency/Recruiter

Office Manager
Northern Cross
RR 1 Box 325
Lecompton, KS 66050
(913) 887-6010
Specialty: G
Employment Agency/Recruiter

Office Manager
Office Mates 5
9401 Indian Creek Pkwy
Shawnee Mission, KS 66210
(913) 661-9111
Specialty: G
Employment Agency/Recruiter

Office Manager
Office Mates 5
3400 SW Van Buren Street
Topeka, KS 66611
(913) 267-5430
Specialty: F,H,L,O
Employment Agency/Recruiter

Office Manager
Office Mates 5
8441 E 32nd St N
Wichita, KS 67226
(316) 634-1966
Specialty: G
Employment Agency/Recruiter

Office Manager
PARR & Assoc
6405 Metcalf Ave
Shawnee Mission, KS 66202
(913) 677-1555
Specialty: G
Employment Agency/Recruiter

Office Manager
Patti Bossert
400 SW Croix Place
Topeka, KS 66611
(913) 267-9999
Specialty: G
Employment Agency/Recruiter

Office Manager
Personametrics Inc
125 N Market St
Wichita, KS 67202
(316) 267-1267
Specialty: G
Employment Agency/Recruiter

Office Manager
Premiere Staffing
7719 Parallel Pky
Kansas City, KS 66112
(913) 299-2111
Specialty: G
Employment Agency/Recruiter

Office Manager
Personnel Services Inc
301 N Main St
Wichita, KS 67202
(316) 264-1515
Specialty: G
Employment Agency/Recruiter

Office Manager
Private Industry Council
3601 S W 29th Ste 127
Topeka, KS 66614
(913) 271-8787
(913) 271-8791 FAX
Specialty: G
Employment Agency/Recruiter

Office Manager
Personnel Solutions Inc
11050 Roe Ave
Shawnee Mission, KS 66211
(913) 345-0505
Specialty: G
Employment Agency/Recruiter

Office Manager
Professional Employment Services Inc
2921 SW Wanamaker Drive
Topeka, KS 66614
(913) 273-5588
Specialty: L,O,S,Food Service, Technical,Professional
Employment Agency/Recruiter

Office Manager
Preferred Medical Placement
815 S Clairborne Rd
Olathe, KS 66062
(913) 780-6845
Specialty: H
Employment Agency/Recruiter

Office Manager
Professional Search
4400 W 109th St
Shawnee Mission, KS 66211
(913) 491-5550
Specialty: G
Employment Agency/Recruiter

Employment Agencies/Recruiters

Office Manager
Robert Half
10955 Lowell Ave Ste 490
Overland Park, KS 66210
(913) 451-7600
Specialty: G
Employment Agency/Recruiter

Office Manager
Rollheiser & Assoc
7101 College Blvd
Shawnee Mission, KS 66210
(913) 661-0133
Specialty: G
Employment Agency/Recruiter

Office Manager
Sales Consultants
9401 Indian Creek Pkwy
Shawnee Mission, KS 66210
(913) 661-9200
Specialty: S
Employment Agency/Recruiter

Office Manager
Sales Consultants
8441 E 32nd St N
Wichita, KS 67226
(316) 634-1981
Specialty: S
Employment Agency/Recruiter

Office Manager
Scully & Assoc Inc
229 S Baltimore Ave
Derby, KS 67307
(316) 788-5885
Specialty: G
Employment Agency/Recruiter

Office Manager
Scully & Associates Inc
P O Box 780885
Wichita, KS 67278
(316) 788-5885
Specialty: G
Employment Agency/Recruiter

Office Manager
Senior Employment Ctr
2501 N 14th Ave
Dodge City, KS 67801
(316) 227-9330
Specialty: G
Employment Agency/Recruiter

Office Manager
Senior Employment Program
100 N Main St Ste 816
Hutchinson, KS 67501
(316) 663-7341
Specialty: G
Employment Agency/Recruiter

Office Manager
SER Corp Jobs For Progress
304 N Main St
Garden City, KS 67846
(316) 275-2181
Specialty: G
Employment Agency/Recruiter

Office Manager
Signature Staffing Inc
6800 College Blvd
Shawnee Mission, KS 66211
(913) 338-2020
Specialty: G
Employment Agency/Recruiter

Office Manager
Source EDP
10300 W 103rd St
Overland Park, KS 66202
(316) 688-1621
Specialty: C
Employment Agency/Recruiter

Office Manager
Source Finance
10300 W 103rd St
Wycliff Office Center
Shawnee Mission, KS 66214
(913) 888-3054
Specialty: G
Employment Agency/Recruiter

David Thorell, Pres
Staffing Solutions Inc
8101 College Blvd Ste 160
Overland Park, KS 66210
(913) 661-0066
(913) 661-0066 FAX
Specialty: C,F,O,S
Employment Agency/Recruiter

Office Manager
Starkey Developmental Ctr Inc
144 S Young St
Wichita, KS 67209
(316) 942-4221
Specialty: G
Employment Agency/Recruiter

Office Manager
Stoneburner Associates
10000 W 75th St
Shawnee Mission, KS 66204
(913) 432-0055
Specialty: G
Employment Agency/Recruiter

Office Manager
Synstrata Corp Inc
8100 E 22nd St N Bldg 500
Wichita, KS 67226
(316) 681-5100
Specialty: G
Employment Agency/Recruiter

Employment Agencies/Recruiters

Office Manager
The Chapple Group Inc
113 N Handley Street
Wichita, KS 67203
(316) 262-2131
Specialty: G
Employment Agency/Recruiter

Office Manager
TOP Personnel Services
11900 College Blvd
Shawnee Mission, KS 66210
(913) 469-1400
Specialty: G
Employment Agency/Recruiter

Office Manager
Topeka Youth Project
1100 SW Gage Blvd
Topeka, KS 66604
(913) 273-4141
Specialty: G
Employment Agency/Recruiter

Office Manager
Wayne-Keith-Simpson Intl
8512 Hallet St
Shawnee Mission, KS 66215
(913) 599-3404
Specialty: G
Employment Agency/Recruiter

Office Manager
White & Assoc
10000 W 75th St Ste 118
Shawnee Mission, KS 66204
(913) 831-1821
Specialty: G
Employment Agency/Recruiter

Office Manager
Wichita Services Inc
2901 Burlingame Rd
Topeka, KS 66611
(913) 683-7336
Specialty: G
Employment Agency/Recruiter

Office Manager
William Lawrence & Assoc
125 N Market St
Wichita, KS 67202
(316) 269-4010
Specialty: G
Employment Agency/Recruiter

Office Manager
Work Options
1611 N Mosley St
Wichita, KS 67214
(316) 264-6604
Specialty: G
Employment Agency/Recruiter

Office Manager
Wright Business School
9500 Marshall Dr
Shawnee Mission, KS 66215
(913) 492-2888
Specialty: G
Employment Agency/Recruiter

Office Manager
WSA Corp
11933 Johnson Dr
Shawnee Mission, KS 66216
(913) 631-3800
Specialty: G
Employment Agency/Recruiter

Office Manager
Wyatt & Associates Inc
9415 E Harry St
Wichita, KS 67207
(316) 682-6740
Specialty: G
Employment Agency/Recruiter

Office Manager
**YWCA Employment &
Resource Network-Earn**
350 N Market St
Wichita, KS 67202
(316) 263-7501
Specialty: G
Employment Agency/Recruiter

Susan R Kelly, Program Director
**YWCA Career Assistance
Network**
225 SW 12th Street
Topeka, KS 66612
(913) 232-8265
(913) 233-4867 FAX
Specialty: C,G,M
Employment Agency/Recruiter

Employment Agencies/Recruiters - Nebraska

The following pages contain the specialty cross-reference listings to an alphabetical list of active employment agencies/recruiters located in Nebraska.

The alphabetical listing is immediately after the cross-reference list.

INDEX CROSS REFERENCE BY SPECIALTY

Specialty: A
(Advertising)

Bellevue Personnel

Specialty: B
(Banking)

Eggers Consulting Company
Management Recruiters
    International
Professions
Robert Half of Omaha

Specialty: C
(Computers & Data Processing)

Bellevue Personnel
Careers By Choice
Celebrity Services
CompuSearch
Contracted Services
Database Resources Inc
Eggers Consulting Company
Management Recruiters
    International
Personnel Search
Probe International Inc
Professions
Reliable
Robert Half of Omaha

Specialty: E
(Engineering)

Bellevue Personnel
Careers By Choice
Eggers Consulting Company
Jordan Palmer & Associates
Management Recruiters
    International
Recruiters International Inc
Reliable

Specialty: F
(Finance & Accounting)

Accounting Resources
American Association Finance
Bellevue Personnel
Career Advance
Careers By Choice
Celebrity Services
CompuSearch
Eggers Consulting Company
Mid America Placement Service
Office Mates 5
Personnel Search
Peters Personnel
Professions
Reliable
Robert Half of Omaha

Employment Agencies/Recruiters

**Specialty: G
(General Applications)**

A & C Personnel Inc
A B C Employment Services
AARP Senior Employment Svc
Able Personnel Service
Accounting Recruiters
Adamy Personnel
Associated Personnel Svc
Barbara Lammers Personnel
    Service
Betty's Bunch Inc
Career Center Inc
Career Design Inc
Career Management Services
CenCor Temporary
Corporate Recruiters
Don Pariset Associates
Dunhill Professional Search
    of Southwest Omaha
Dunhill Search of Omaha Inc
Express Services
Guaranteed Placement Services
Hansen Employment &
    Counseling Services
Harlan J Rohrberg
Help Inc
Hohlfeld Employment Svc
Home Care & Companions Inc
Interim Services Inc
J Douglas Scott & Associates
Job Training Dept-Labor
Kenneth Mertins
Lincoln Personnel Svc
Management Recruiters
Management Recruiters
    International

Marjorie Rohrberg
McKenzie & Michaels Inc
MSP Resources Inc
Nebraska Green Thumb
New Beginnings
Noll Executive Search
Office Mates 5
Olsten Temporary Svc
Omaha Temporary Svc
Operation Able For 50+
    Job Seekers
Personnel Leasing
Professional Med Temps
Professional Personnel
    Services Inc
Professional Recruiter Inc
Professional Resources
    Management
Quest Personnel
Sales Consultants
Sanford Rose Associates
Scott J Douglas & Associates
Search America
Search International
Sherri Kunz CPC
Snelling & Snelling
Staff Mid-America
Tys Employment Service
Veterans Employment Info
Wilson Consulting

**Specialty: H
(Healthcare)**

Bellevue Personnel
Health Service Professionals

Management Recruiters
    International
Personnel Search
Peters Personnel
Professions

Specialty: I
(Insurance)

Bellevue Personnel
Eggers Consulting Company
Insurance Placement
Management Recruiters
    International
Professions

Specialty: L
(Legal)

Office Mates 5

Specialty: M
(Manufacturing)

Management Recruiters
    International

Specialty: O
(Office Administration)

Bellevue Personnel
Celebrity Services
Eggers Consulting Company
Mid America Placement Service

Office Mates 5
Peters Personnel
Recruiters International Inc
Reliable

Specialty: P
(Personnel & Human Resources)

Management Recruiters
    International
Office Mates 5
Peters Personnel

Specialty: R
(Research & Development)

Management Recruiters
    International

Specialty: S
(Sales & Marketing)

Bellevue Personnel
Career Advance
Eggers Consulting Company
Management Recruiters
    International
Mid America Placement Service
Office Mates 5
Professions
Recruiters International Inc
Reliable
Sales Recruiters

**Specialty: T
(Travel, Food & Hospitality)**

Bellevue Personnel
Career Advance

OTHER SPECIFIC SPECIALTIES:

Specialty: Agricultural

Agri-Associates
Eggers Consulting Company

Specialty: Architecture

Reliable

Specialty: Construction

Reliable

Specialty: Food Service

Mid America Placement Service

Specialty: Retail

Bellevue Personnel
Career Advance
Eggers Consulting Company
Mid America Placement Service

Specialty: Technical

Bellevue Personnel
Eggers Consulting Company
Jordan Palmer & Associates
Mid America Placement Service
Recruiters International Inc

Specialty: Telecom

Bellevue Personnel

Office Manager
A & C Personnel Inc
8601 W Dodge Road Ste 31
Omaha, NE 68114
(402) 393-4707
Specialty: G
Employment Agency/Recruiter

Office Manager
A B C Employment Services
770 N Cotner Blvd
Lincoln, NE 68505
(402) 467-537
Specialty: G
Employment Agency/Recruiter

Office Manager
AARP Senior Employment Svc
315 S 9th St Ste 12
Lincoln, NE 68508
(402) 475-3283
Specialty: G
Employment Agency/Recruiter

Office Manager
Able Personnel Service
213 S 1 Suite F
Norfolk, NE 68701
(402) 379-2939
Specialty: G
Employment Agency/Recruiter

Office Manager
Accounting Recruiters
5301 S 144 Street
Omaha, NE 68137
(402) 896-9494
Specialty: G
Employment Agency/Recruiter

Office Manager
Accounting Resources
8744 Federick Street
Omaha, NE 68124
(402) 397-3308
Specialty: F
Employment Agency/Recruiter

Office Manager
Adamy Personnel
2718 16th St
Columbus, NE 68601
(402) 563-2101
Specialty: G
Employment Agency/Recruiter

Office Manager
Agri-Associates
10330 Regency Parkway Drive
Omaha, NE 68114
(402) 397-4410
Specialty: Agricultural
Employment Agency/Recruiter

Employment Agencies/Recruiters 107

Office Manager
American Association Finance
1126 S 72nd St
Omaha, NE 68124
(402) 392-1980
Specialty: F
Employment Agency/Recruiter

Office Manager
Associated Personnel Svc
1220 E Capital Ave
Grand Island, NE 68801
(308) 384-4885
Specialty: G
Employment Agency/Recruiter

Office Manager
Barbara Lammers Personnel Service
7117 Farnam Street
Omaha, NE 68132
(402) 397-1500
Specialty: G
Employment Agency/Recruiter

Office Manager
Bellevue Personnel
1820 Hillcrest Drive Ste F
Bellevue, NE 68005
(402) 291-6611
Specialty: A,C,E,F,H,I,O,S,T, Retail, Telecom, Technical
Employment Agency/Recruiter

Office Manager
Betty's Bunch Inc
231 N 1st St Ste 4
Seward, NE 68434
(402) 643-2809
Specialty: G
Employment Agency/Recruiter

Office Manager
Career Advance
8801 W Center Road Ste 204
Omaha, NE 68124
(402) 392-1900
Specialty: F,S,T,Retail
Employment Agency/Recruiter

Office Manager
Career Center Inc
7602 Pacific St LL 103
Omaha, NE 68114
(402) 399-2070
Specialty: G
Employment Agency/Recruiter

Office Manager
Career Design Inc
12020 Shamrock Plaza #300
Omaha, NE 68154
(402) 333-8484
Specialty: G
Employment Agency/Recruiter

Vaughn L Carter, Pres
Career Management Services
5000 Central Park Drive Ste 204
Lincoln, NE 68504
(402) 466-8427
(402) 466-5933 FAX
Specialty: G
Employment Agency/Recruiter

Office Manager
CenCor Temporary
7000 W Center Rd Ste 218
Omaha, NE 68106
(402) 393-5844
Specialty: G
Employment Agency/Recruiter

Office Manager
Careers By Choice
6675 Redick Ave Ste A
Omaha, NE 68152
(402) 571-8140
Specialty: C,E,F
Employment Agency/Recruiter

Jean Felton, Admin Manager
CompuSearch
210 Gateway Ste 434
Lincoln, NE 68505
(402) 467-5549
Specialty: C,F
Employment Agency/Recruiter

Office Manager
Celebrity Services
210 S 16th Street
Omaha, NE 68102
(402) 345-2434
Specialty: C,F,O
Employment Agency/Recruiter

Office Manager
CompuSearch
7171 Mercy Road
Omaha, NE 68106
(402) 397-8115
Specialty: C
Employment Agency/Recruiter

Office Manager
Celebrity Services
1126 South 72nd Street
Omaha, NE 68124
(402) 393-0404
Specialty: C,F,O
Employment Agency/Recruiter

Brita M Castrop, Development
Contracted Services
11635 Arbor Street
Omaha, NE 68144
(402) 333-1700
Specialty: C(contract services)
Contract Services Firm

Employment Agencies/Recruiters

Office Manager
Corporate Recruiters
202 S 71st St Ste F
Omaha, NE 68132
(402) 393-5515
Specialty: G
Employment Agency/Recruiter

Office Manager
Database Resources Inc
1674 S 153rd Street
Omaha, NE 68144
(402) 330-9908
Specialty: C
Employment Agency/Recruiter

Office Manager
Don Pariset Associates
1525 S 106 St
Omaha, NE 68124
(402) 397-7092
Specialty: G
Employment Agency/Recruiter

Office Manager
**Dunhill Professional Search
of Southwest Omaha**
7500 Main Street
Ralton, NE 68127
(402) 331-1644
Specialty: G
Employment Agency/Recruiter

Office Manager
Dunhill Search of Omaha Inc
13426 A Street
Omaha, NE 68144
(402) 334-1233
Specialty: G
Employment Agency/Recruiter

Office Manager
Eggers Consulting Company
11272 Elm Street
Omaha, NE 68144
(402) 333-3480
(402) 333-9759 FAX
Specialty: B,C,E,F,I,O,S,Retail,
Agricultural,Technical
Employment Agency/Recruiter

Office Manager
Express Services
6031 S 58 St Ste C
Lincoln, NE 68516
(402) 421-2100
Specialty: G
Employment Agency/Recruiter

Office Manager
Guaranteed Placement Services
310 N 115 Street
Omaha, NE 68154
(402) 333-3430
(402) 333-3378 FAX
Specialty: G
Employment Agency/Recruiter

Office Manager
Hansen Employment & Counseling Services
2608 West Old Fair Road
Grand Island, NE 68803
(308) 382-7350
Specialty: G
Employment Agency/Recruiter

Office Manager
Harlan J Rohrberg
11318 Davenport Street
Omaha, NE 68154
(402) 330-2814
Specialty: G
Employment Agency/Recruiter

Office Manager
Health Service Professinals
202 S 71st Street
Omaha, NE 68132
(402) 393-5515
Specialty: H
Employment Agency/Recruiter

Office Manager
Help Inc
13911 Gold Circle
Omaha, NE 68144
(402) 333-2333
Specialty: G
Employment Agency/Recruiter

Office Manager
Hohlfeld Employment Svc
105 N Hastings Ave
Hastings, NE 68901
(402) 462-2101
Specialty: G
Employment Agency/Recruiter

Office Manager
Home Care & Companions Inc
2121 N Webb Rd Ste 307
Grand Island, NE 68803
(308) 382-3436
Specialty: G
Employment Agency/Recruiter

Office Manager
Insurance Placement
808 P Street
Haymarket Square
Lincoln, NE 68508
(402) 476-2200
Specialty: I
Employment Agency/Recruiter

Office Manager
Interim Services Inc
233 N 48th St Ste U
Lincoln, NE 68504
(402) 466-1996
Specialty: G
Employment Agency/Recruiter

Employment Agencies/Recruiters 111

Office Manager
J Douglas Scott & Associates
7171 Mercy Road
Omaha, NE 68106
(402) 393-3905
Specialty: G
Employment Agency/Recruiter

Office Manager
Job Training Dept-Labor
520 Lincoln Ave
York, NE 68467
(402) 362-7628
Specialty: G
Employment Agency/Recruiter

Office Manager
Jordan Palmer & Associates
P O Box 24106
Omaha, NE 68124
(402) 392-2885
Specialty: E,Technical
Employment Agency/Recruiter

Office Manager
Kenneth Mertins
11330 Q Street
Omaha, NE 68137
(402) 339-9839
Specialty: G
Employment Agency/Recruiter

Office Manager
Lincoln Personnel Svc
4706 S 48th
Lincoln, NE 68516
(402) 489-9055
Specialty: G
Employment Agency/Recruiter

Office Manager
Management Recruiters
7171 Mercy Road
Omaha, NE 68106
(402) 397-8320
Specialty: G
Employment Agency/Recruiter

Jean Felton, Admin Manager
Management Recruiters International
210 Gateway Ste 434
Lincoln, NE 68505
(402) 467-5534
Specialty: B,C,E,F,G,H,I,M,P,R,S,
Employment Agency/Recruiter

Office Manager
Marjorie Rohrberg
11318 Davenport St
Omaha, NE 68154
(402) 330-2814
Specialty: G
Employment Agency/Recruiter

Office Manager
McKenzie & Michaels Inc
12020 Shamrock Plaza
Omaha, NE 68154
(402) 334-7494
Specialty: G
Employment Agency/Recruiter

Office Manager
New Beginnings
1211 Main Ave
Crete, NE 68333
(402) 826-2728
Specialty: G
Employment Agency/Recruiter

Office Manager
Mid America Placement Service
4001 Center Street Ste 520
Omaha, NE 68105
(402) 341-3338
Specialty: F,O,S,Technical,
Food Service, Retail
Employment Agency/Recruiter

Office Manager
Noll Executive Search
900 Commercial Federal Tower
Omaha, NE 68124
(402) 391-7736
Specialty: G
Employment Agency/Recruiter

Office Manager
MSP Resources Inc
436 Greentree Ct
Lincoln, NE 68505
(402) 464-3225
Specialty: G
Employment Agency/Recruiter

Jean Felton, Admin Mgr
Office Mates 5
210 Gateway Ste 434
Lincoln, NE 68505
(402) 467-5534
Specialty: F,G,L,O,P,S,Clerical
Employment Agency/Recruiter

Office Manager
Nebraska Green Thumb
2012 S 13th St
Lincoln, NE 68502
(402) 475-5226
Specialty: G
Employment Agency/Recruiter

Office Manager
Office Mates 5
7171 Mercy Road Ste 252
Omaha, NE 68106
(402) 397-8320
Specialty: F,O
Employment Agency/Recruiter

Employment Agencies/Recruiters

Office Manager
Olsten Temporary Svc
10843 Old Mill Rd
Omaha, NE 68154
(402) 330-5200
Specialty: G
Employment Agency/Recruiter

Office Manager
Omaha Temporary Svc
2066 Farnam St
Omaha, NE 68102
(402) 344-4848
Specialty: G
Employment Agency/Recruiter

Office Manager
**Operation Able For
50+ Job Seekers**
129 N 10 Street Room 236
Lincoln, NE 68508
(402) 441-7064
Specialty: G
Employment Agency/Recruiter

Office Manager
Personnel Leasing
1126 S 72 Street
Omaha, NE 68124
(402) 397-9530
Specialty: G
Employment Agency/Recruiter

Office Manager
Personnel Search
8744 Frederick Street
Omaha, NE 68124
(402) 397-2980
Specialty: C,F,H
Employment Agency/Recruiter

Office Manager
Peters Personnel
2120 S 72 Street Ste 1022
Omaha, NE 68124
(402) 390-9890
Specialty: F,H,O,P
Employment Agency/Recruiter

John R Graco, Pres
Probe International Inc
16252 Riggs Street
Omaha, NE 68135
(402) 896-9300
(402) 896-3534 FAX
Specialty: C
Employment Agency/Recruiter

Office Manager
Professional Med Temps
8601 W Dodge Rd
Omaha, NE 68114
(402) 393-4965
Specialty: G
Employment Agency/Recruiter

Office Manager
Professional Personnel Svc
3201 Pioneers Blvd Ste 222
Lincoln, NE 68502
(402) 483-7821
Specialty: G
Employment Agency/Recruiter

Office Manager
Professional Recruiter Inc
7253 Grover Street
Omaha, NE 68124
(402) 397-2885
Specialty: G
Employment Agency/Recruiter

Office Manager
Professional Resources Management
211 N 12 Street
Lincoln, NE 68508
(402) 476-1011
Specialty: G
Employment Agency/Recruiter

Office Manager
Professions
501 Olson Drive Ste 2
Papillon, NE 68128
(402) 331-6440
(402) 331-8826 FAX
Specialty: B,C,F,H,I,S
Employment Agency/Recruiter

Office Manager
Quest Personnel
3020 N 102 Street
Omaha, NE 68134
(402) 571-4500
Specialty: G
Employment Agency/Recruiter

Office Manager
Recruiters International Inc
11330 Q Street Ste 218
Omaha, NE 68137
(402) 339-9839
Specialty: E,O,S,Technical
Employment Agency/Recruiter

Office Manager
Reliable
11318 Davenport Street
Omaha, NE 68154
(402) 330-2814
(402) 330-8164 FAX
Specialty: C,E,F,O,S, Construction,Architecture
Employment Agency/Recruiter

Office Manager
Robert Half of Omaha
7171 Mercy Road Ste 302
Omaha, NE 68106
(402) 397-8107
Specialty: B,C,F
Employment Agency/Recruiter

Office Manager
Sales Consultants
10855 W Dodge Rd Ste 290
Omaha, NE 68154
(402) 330-4800
Specialty: G
Employment Agency/Recruiter

Office Manager
Sales Recruiters
210 Gateway Mall Ste 434
Gateway, NE 68505
(402) 467-5534
Specialty: S
Employment Agency/Recruiter

Office Manager
Sanford Rose Associates
105 Wedgewood Drive
Lincoln, NE 68510
(402) 486-3116
Specialty: G
Employment Agency/Recruiter

Office Manager
Scott J Douglas & Associates
7171 Mercy Rd
Omaha, NE 68106
(402) 393-3905
Specialty: G
Employment Agency/Recruiter

Office Manager
Search America
Rt 2 Box 120
Blair, NE 68008
(402) 339-0888
Specialty: G
Employment Agency/Recruiter

Office Manager
Search International
3020 N 102 Street
Omaha, NE 68134
(402) 571-4511
Specialty: G
Employment Agency/Recruiter

Office Manager
Sherri Kunz CPC
P O Box 24106
Omaha, NE 68124
(402) 393-2885
Specialty: G
Employment Agency/Recruiter

Office Manager
Snelling & Snelling
13304 W Center Road
Omaha, NE 68144
(402) 330-0100
Specialty: G
Employment Agency/Recruiter

Office Manager
Staff Mid-America
7602 Pacific Street
Lower Level Ste 100
Omaha, NE 68114
(402) 391-2065
Specialty: G
Employment Agency/Recruiter

Office Manager
Tys Employment Service
11225 Davenport Street
Omaha, NE 68154
(402) 333-6356
Specialty: G
Employment Agency/Recruiter

Office Manager
Veterans Employment Info
406 E 6 St
Fremont, NE 68025
(308) 727-3250
Specialty: G
Employment Agency/Recruiter

Office Manager
Wilson Consulting
Suite 218 Center Bldg
Omaha, NE 68105
(402) 341-2551
Specialty: G
Employment Agency/Recruiter

Employment Agencies/Recruiters - North Dakota

The following pages contain the specialty cross-reference listings to an alphabetical list of active employment agencies/recruiters located in North Dakota.

The alphabetical listing is immediately after the cross-reference list.

INDEX CROSS REFERENCE BY SPECIALTY

Specialty: C
(Computers & Data Processing)

The Career Connection

Specialty: E
(Engineering)

The Career Connection

Specialty: F
(Finance & Accounting)

The Career Connection

Specialty: G
(General Applications)

Career Network
Community Enterprise
Dial A Job
Employment Opportunities
Expressway Personnel
Garrison Area Improvement
    Association
Great Plains Benefit Grp
Green Thumb Inc
Image Builders Consulting
Job Service North Dakota
JobNet
Midwest Farm Worker
    Employment & Training

Midwest Farmworker
    Employment
North Dakota Job Svc
Personnel Services Inc
Preference Personnel
Preferred Temporary Svc
Shafer Employment
Snelling And Snelling
Staff Pros
Success Unlimited Inc

Specialty: M
(Manufacturing)

The Career Connection

OTHER SPECIFIC SPECIALTIES:

Specialty: Farmworkers

Midwest Farmworker
    Employment & Training

Employment Agencies/Recruiters

Office Manager
Career Network
1131 Westrac Dr Ste 202
Fargo, ND 58103
(701) 237-6931
Specialty: G
Employment Agency/Recruiter

Office Manager
Career Network
1407 24th Ave S Ste 217
Grand Forks, ND 58201
(701) 775-2808
Specialty: G
Employment Agency/Recruiter

Office Manager
Community Enterprise
515 E Main Ave
Bismarck, ND 58501
(701) 258-8564
Specialty: G
Employment Agency/Recruiter

Office Manager
Dial A Job
512 Black Bldg
Fargo, ND 58102
(701) 237-9591
Specialty: G
Employment Agency/Recruiter

Office Manager
Employment Opportunities
409 Main St
Williston, ND 58801
(701) 572-6003
Specialty: G
Employment Agency/Recruiter

Office Manager
Expressway Personnel
523 E Bismarck Expy
Bismarck, ND 58504
(701) 222-0071
Specialty: G
Employment Agency/Recruiter

Office Manager
Garrison Area Improvement Association
142 Main N
Garrison, ND 59540
(701) 463-2631
Specialty: G
Employment Agency/Recruiter

Office Manager
Great Plains Benefit Grp
523 E Bismarck Expy
Bismarck, ND 58504
(701) 258-0039
Specialty: G
Employment Agency/Recruiter

Office Manager
Green Thumb Inc
1424 W Century Ave
Bismarck, ND 58501
(701) 258-8879
Specialty: G
Employment Agency/Recruiter

Karen Solhjem
Image Builders Consulting
133 West Main Box 265
West Fargo, ND 58078
(701) 277-1650
Specialty: G
Employment Agency/Recruiter

Office Manager
Job Service
119 9th St W
Harvey, ND 58341
(701) 324-4552
Specialty: G
Employment Agency/Recruiter

Office Manager
Job Service North Dakota
1350 32nd St SW
Fargo, ND 58103
(701) 239-7300
Specialty: G
Employment Agency/Recruiter

Office Manager
Job Service North Dakota
3416 B Broadway
Minot, ND 58701
(605) 857-7650
(800) 482-0017
Specialty: G
Employment Agency/Recruiter

Office Manager
JobNet
109 1/2 Broadway St N
Fargo, ND 58102
(701) 237-9262
Specialty: G
Employment Agency/Recruiter

Office Manager
Midwest Farm Worker Employment & Training
533 Airport Rd Ste E
Bismarck, ND 58504
(701) 223-4700
Specialty: G
Employment Agency/Recruiter

Office Manager
Midwest Farmworker Employment
1323 23rd St S
Fargo, ND 58103
(701) 293-5959
Specialty: G
Employment Agency/Recruiter

Employment Agencies/Recruiters 121

Office Manager
**Midwest Farmworker
Employment & Training Inc**
21 S Main
Minot, ND 58701
(605) 838-6740
Specialty: Farmworkers
Employment Agency/Recruiter

Office Manager
North Dakota Job Svc
301 College Dr S
Devils Lake, ND 58301
(701) 662-2181
Specialty: G
Employment Agency/Recruiter

Office Manager
Personnel Services Inc
401 S Main
Minot, ND 58701
(605) 852-2038
(605) 852-8614 FAX
Specialty: G
Employment Agency/Recruiter

Office Manager
Preference Personnel
1351 Page Dr SW
Fargo, ND 58103
(701) 293-6905
Specialty: G
Employment Agency/Recruiter

Office Manager
Preferred Temporary Svc
1351 Page Dr Ste 108
Fargo, ND 58103
(701) 293-9349
Specialty: G
Employment Agency/Recruiter

Office Manager
Shafer Employment
512 Black Bldg
Fargo, ND 58102
(701) 237-9495
Specialty: G
Employment Agency/Recruiter

Office Manager
Snelling & Snelling
609 1/2 1st Ave N
Fargo, ND 58102
(701) 237-0600
Specialty: G
Employment Agency/Recruiter

Doug Keller
Snelling And Snelling
433 E Bismarck Expy Ste 4
Bismark, ND 58504
(701) 222-1144
Specialty: G
Employment Agency/Recruiter

Office Manager
Staff Pros
540 6th Ave N
Fargo, ND 58102
(701) 235-7551
Specialty: G
Employment Agency/Recruiter

Office Manager
Success Unlimited Inc
2524 Washington St S
Grand Forks, ND 58204
(701) 775-3356
Specialty: G
Employment Agency/Recruiter

Twila F Deahl, Owner
The Career Connection
1621 S University Drive Ste 215
Fargo, ND 58103
(701) 232-4614
(701) 241-9822 FAX
Specialty: C,E,F,M
Employment Agency/Recruiter

Employment Agencies/Recruiters - South Dakota

The following pages contain the specialty cross-reference listings to an alphabetical list of active employment agencies/recruiters located in South Dakota.

The alphabetical listing is immediately after the cross-reference list.

INDEX CROSS REFERENCE BY SPECIALTY

Specialty B:
(Banking)

Metro Personnel Services

Specialty: C
(Computers & Data Processing)

Metro Personnel Services
Snelling Personnel Services

Specialty: E
(Engineering)

Metro Personnel Services
Snelling Personnel Services

Specialty: F
(Finance & Accounting)

Action Temporary &
    Personnel Inc
Metro Personnel Services
Snelling Personnel Services

Specialty: G
(General Applications)

Andrew's Alternative Human
    Resource

Availability Employment
Careers Unlimited
Express Services
Interim Healthcare
Interim Staff Pros
Interstate Personnel Service
Job Service of South Dakota
Langerud Career Specialists Inc
Management Recruiters
Mari D's Services Unlimited
Nettleton Junior College
Olsten Temporary Services
Snelling & Snelling
United Sioux Tribes
    Development Corp
Weaver Jones & Company Inc

Specialty: H
(Healthcare)

Action Temporary &
    Personnel Inc

Specialty: L
(Legal)

Action Temporary &
    Personnel Inc

Specialty: M
(Manufacturing)

Snelling Personnel Services

Specialty: O
(Office Administration)

Metro Personnel Services
Snelling Personnel Services

Specialty: S
(Sales & Marketing)

Metro Personnel Services
Snelling Personnel Services

Specialty: T
(Travel, Food & Hospitality)

Snelling Personnel Services

OTHER SPECIFIC SPECIALTIES:

Specialty: Management

Metro Personnel Services
Snelling Personnel Services

Specialty: Technical

Snelling Personnel Services

Office Manager
Action Temporary & Personnel Inc
1010 W 41st Street
Sioux Falls, SD 57105
(605) 338-6465
Specialty: F,H,L,O
Employment Agency/Recruiter

Office Manager
Andrew's Alternative Human Resource
408 S 2nd Ave
Sioux Falls, SD 57102
(605) 335-8198
Specialty: G
Employment Agency/Recruiter

Office Manager
Availability Employment
1521 S Minnesota Avenue
Sioux Falls, SD 57105
(605) 336-0353
Specialty: G
Employment Agency/Recruiter

Office Manager
Careers Unlimited
3401 S Kelley
Sioux Falls, SD 57116
(605) 361-9820
Specialty: G
Employment Agency/Recruiter

Office Manager
Express Services
923 6th Avenue SE
Aberdeen, SD 57401
(605) 225-9222
Specialty: G
Employment Agency/Recruiter

Office Manager
Interim Healthcare
2520 W 41st St
Sioux Falls, SD 57105
(605) 332-3939
Specialty: G
Employment Agency/Recruiter

Office Manager
Interim Staff Pros
300 N Dakota Avenue Ste 104
Sioux Falls, SD 57102
(605) 335-6010
Specialty: G
Employment Agency/Recruiter

Office Manager
Interstate Personnel Service
P O Box 1167
North Sioux City, SD 57049
(605) 232-9119
Specialty: G
Employment Agency/Recruiter

Employment Agencies/Recruiters

Office Manager
Job Service of South Dakota
120 W 2nd Street
Miller, SD 57362
(605) 853-3117
Specialty: G
Employment Agency/Recruiter

Deanna Langerud, Pres
Langerud Career Specialists Inc
909 St Joseph Street Ste 555
P O Box 8321
Rapid City, SD 57709-8321
(605) 341-0885
(605) 341-3306 FAX
Specialty: G
Employment Agency/Recruiter

Office Manager
Management Recruiters
2600 S Minnesota Avenue
Sioux Falls, SD 57105
(605) 334-9291
Specialty: G
Employment Agency/Recruiter

Office Manager
Mari D's Services Unlimited
122 S Roosevelt Street
Aberdeen, SD 57401
(605) 229-0094
Specialty: G
Employment Agency/Recruiter

Office Manager
Metro Personnel Services
812 S Minnesota Avenue
Sioux Falls, SD 57104
(605) 334-1000
(605) 334-0159 FAX
Specialty: B,C,E,F,O,S,
Management
Employment Agency/Recruiter

Office Manager
Nettleton Junior College
100 S Spring Ave
Sioux Falls, SD 57104
(605) 336-1837
Specialty: G
Employment Agency/Recruiter

Office Manager
Olsten Temporary Services
333 Sheffer St
Rapid City, SD 57702
(605) 348-8010
Specialty: G
Employment Agency/Recruiter

Office Manager
Snelling & Snelling
2525 W Main Street Ste 301
Rapid City, SD 57702
(605) 341-4111
Specialty: G
Employment Agency/Recruiter

Office Manager
Snelling Personnel Services
2720 W 12th Street Ste 200
Sioux Falls, SD 57104
(605) 334-1434
Specialty: C,E,F,M,O,S,T,
Technical, Management
Employment Agency/Recruiter

Office Manager
**United Sioux Tribes
Development Corp**
422 5th Avenue SE
Aberdeen, SD 57401
(605) 225-9513
Specialty: G
Employment Agency/Recruiter

Office Manager
Weaver Jones & Company Inc
P O Box 7594
Rapid City, SD 57709
(605) 341-7455
Specialty: G
Employment Agency/Recruiter

JOB SEEKERS SURVIVAL HINTS

Effectively work through the help wanted section of the newspaper to prospect for new job openings.

Use the following helpful hints to aid you in this area:

- Don't delay -- Get the newspaper everyday. If your city has both a morning and evening paper, then get both of them.

- Develop a system for marking each ad -- Circle or highlight all new ads. Mark through those ads that you have no interest in with an "X". For ads that you have previously responded to, mark through them with a " / ". This exercise will cause you to focus your attention on every ad so that no new ones of interest are overlooked.

- Consider all ads important -- Don't skip over ads just because they are short such as "Shipping Manager, Send resume or call". Assume that each has a hidden value worthy of a response or at least checking out further.

- Prioritize the new ads according to interest -- Group the new ads by marking them with a "1" for those of interest and a "2" for those that are 'Maybes' and a "3" for those that need further information.

- <u>Respond promptly</u> -- Create a cover letter tailored to present your credentials in the best form to meet the needs expressed in the ad. If you lack some of the specific qualification required, respond by substituting practical experience either in the field described or a collateral field. However you respond, do it quickly. Each response should have a typo free signed cover letter accompanied by a crisp clean copy of your resume.

- <u>Track your responses</u> -- Create an alphabetical file of new ads responded to. Keep a copy of your cover letter in a separate alphabetical file for quick reference for when you are contacted.

PLAINS STATES JOB SEEKERS SOURCEBOOK

Section 5

Executive Recruiters

Executive Recruiters Defined

Executive Recruiters usually perform exclusive searches for positions that pay from $50,000 to several hundred thousand dollars per year. These firms are compensated by a hiring company to locate a person with specific qualifications to meet a predefined employment need.

The major executive search firms conduct searches for hiring companies on an exclusive retainer basis. This means that the search firm is paid for their efforts even if they are not successful in filling the position. Firms that work on a contingency basis are paid only if an acceptable candidate is found and hired by the hiring company.

Since many of the executive search firms work on a retainer basis, getting in to see one can sometimes be difficult. However, it is worth the effort to reach these firms since these industry specialists know the job market extremely well and can be helpful in providing advice as well as leads. An executive seeking total exposure should touch base with all executive search firms both contingency and retainer.

Neither type of firm should charge the individual; all fees are paid by the hiring company. Firms that charge fees to an individual are not typical and it is best to avoid them.

The value of an executive recruiter to a job seeker depends upon several things: the quality of the agency, the kind of work being sought, and your own level of experience. A good executive recruiter will help its candidates develop a strategy and prepare for personal interviews.

More and more executive recruiters are taking advantage of computer automation and professional affiliations to share both candidate and job order information with other recruiters, making such firms more beneficial to a both job seekers and hiring companies.

To assist you, we have filled the next few pages with important information which will be helpful in understanding how to:

- Select an Executive Recruiter

- Work with an Executive Recruiter

How to Select an
Executive Recruiter

Finding the right executive recruiter to help you find a job or change jobs requires some careful research on your part.

This is an important process that cannot and should not be ignored. Also, this process is slightly different than the process used to select an employment agency, because for the most part executive recruiters are usually retained by hiring companies to fill specific management and staff positions that average salaries of over $50,000.

To maximize your chances of obtaining a job by contacting executive recruiters requires that you work hard to qualify and then select recruiters that want to represent you in your job search. To assist you in this selection process we've outlined some important selection criteria that should be useful.

Selection Criteria:

The selection of the right executive search firm to support your job search efforts should be based upon a combination of the following criteria:

Specialty   Does the firm specialize in making placements in your career field and industry?

If so, this firm is more likely to be able to help find you a new job. If it deals exclusively in your discipline, so much the better.

Proximity   Is the firm convenient for you to visit on a regular basis?

This is important when attempting to maintain high visibility with an individual recruiter.

Experience How long has the firm and the recruiter been in the placement business? And how long has the firm been making placements for members of your profession?

It is best to select a recruiter who has at least three years experience specializing in your industry. These recruiters will already have established a network of contacts with a number of hiring companies and will be better sources for new job openings.

Personality Does the recruiter like you and do you like the recruiter? Are you comfortable with the recruiter's business style and ability to represent you to hiring companies?

This is very important if you want to have a better shot at establishing and maintaining a good rapport with the recruiter on an ongoing basis.

Referrals   Was this firm referred to you by someone else in your field?

Added to the positive responses for the preceding qualifiers, a referral will give you an edge over other job seekers.

Quality   Does this recruiter have a good reputation and do they present themselves in a professional manner?

The best way to determine this is to talk to other job seekers and to visit the recruiter's office to obtain personal knowledge of the company image and how it works. If you're unhappy with what you see or find, keep looking.

Networks   Is this executive recruiter a member of a placement affiliation or shared database network?

If yes, then the chances are better that this firm will give you broader exposure to the employment market.

Most reputable firms belong to an organization titled the Association of Executive Recruiting Consultants (AERC).

Attitude   Does this executive recruiter demonstrate that he/she can be helpful in finding you a position?

If not, then continue to contact other executive recruiters until you find one who thinks that he/she can help you.

Questions to ask to qualify an executive recruiter:

1. How long have they been in the placement business?

   The longer a firm has been in the business, the more contacts they are likely to have, therefore the odds of the firm being able to help you are better.

2. How many client companies are they working with?

   While it is difficult to pinpoint an average number that would be about the right size to support you in your job search, if you correlate responses, the differences between firms will be apparent.

   Those firms attempting to handle a larger number of hiring companies per recruiter may be spreading their resources too thin, especially if the number of placements per recruiter is low.

3. How many job openings are they working on at any one time?

   Ten to fifteen per month is typical for a seasoned recruiter.

4. How many placements have they made (monthly/annually)?

   The average recruiter will make one to two per month.

5. Do they feel that they can help you?

   If not, then keep looking, but also ask the next question.

6. If they can't help you, can they recommend and refer you to someone else who could?

   Use this question to expand your network of contacts. If you can get a referral to another firm, then the odds are that you will increase your chances of getting an interview opportunity and personal attention of the other recruiter.

7. Do they accept resumes and how are the resumes reviewed and handled? Are there specific requirements for candidates?

   Many firms do not work with recent college grads, persons not currently employed, persons not in a specific field for a certain number of years or persons whose earnings don't meet their requirements. If this information is not known you can waste time and money on resumes and cover letters.

Working with an Executive Recruiter

To maximize your success of having an executive recruiter find you a job, you need to remember a few important axioms.

Executive recruiters normally are retained by a hiring company to find a specific type of individual to fill a specific job opening.

This means that unless you fill a current need, chances are recruiters may not be willing to spend too much time with you. First determine whether the firm specializes in positions that fit your background.

If the firm's area of expertise matches your background, then send the firm a current resume along with a targeted cover letter explaining the types of positions that you are qualified for.

Next, try to set an appointment to meet personally with a recruiter to sell yourself and establish a rapport. After this meeting, your next step is to do everything possible to help make the recruiter's job easier. This includes having a very good resume available for their use, and prepared and on time for any job interviews arranged.

Executive recruiters will quickly lose interest in a job applicant that continually turns down job offers.

To prevent problems, be specific with the executive recruiter as to what you are looking for in a company and a position. Do this during your first meeting. Give honest answers as to career goals and salary requirements.

If either the job offer, the position, or the company environment are not right, then by all means turn it down, but discuss it first with your recruiter so he/she understands your reasons. Just remember that you run the risk of losing their support if you turn down too many offers.

 Executive recruiters prefer to have an exclusive commitment from a job seeker.

This means that if you are going to use multiple recruiters to speed up your job search, keep this information to yourself.

The level of interest executive recruiters have in helping you find a job drops to almost zero once they know that you are shopping around.

 Executive recruiters see many people each day in addition to receiving a large number of resumes in the daily mail from job seekers.

This means that you must get noticed and stay noticed by them if you want them to help you. But this must be accomplished without becoming a pest. There are a variety of ways of doing this such as:

1. Hand deliver your resume and spend some time asking questions, answering questions, and establishing a rapport.

2. Call your contact on a weekly basis to update your status and ask for an update on the job market and your specific activity.

3. Send them a thank you note, after your initial meeting to thank them for taking an interest in helping you.

4. Drop by the office once every two weeks to spend a few quick moments with your contact. Avoid Mondays or Fridays, as these days are always their busiest.

5. From time to time, bring a small gift (ie. donuts, candy, etc.) with you when you drop in for a visit.

6. When you come across current articles in newspapers or magazines about company expansions or relocations that could be of interest to your recruiter, clip the article and send it to your recruiter along with a note.

The service executive recruiters provide to job seekers is free, but these recruiters need to make a living too.

Treat them with respect, and be thoughtful enough to at least notify them when you have taken a job offer from another source.

If you were extremely satisfied with their efforts, refer job openings to them as well as other good job seekers. This will allow you to maintain contact with them and keep your options open for some future date when you may need someone to again help you find a job in a timely manner.

If you really appreciated their efforts, send them a thank you card or a little gift to show your appreciation for their efforts. Next time, they'll welcome you with open arms.

Executive recruiters know their job, but they don't know you or how well you can perform your job.

This means that they need your help in getting to know you. Remember, you know your job qualifications and experiences better than anyone, so identify your strong points to them. Describe and classify the important features of previous accomplishments.

Furnish them with a means of measuring performance, such as a list of awards or reference letters.

Be honest about your background or problems. If you're not sure you want to change jobs, let your recruiter know about your uncertainty.

Questions to ask about job openings:

1. How long has the job opening been available?

    If just a short time and you've received an offer, the company involved can make decisions quickly. If the job has been open a long time, ask why, prior to making any acceptance decision.

2. Why wasn't the position filled from within the company?

    If you don't like the answer, then the odds for future promotions within the company may be slim.

3. Why is the job open?

    If someone retired or it's a new position, these are all positive signs. If someone left the company or was terminated, it would be helpful to understand the circumstances prior to making a long term commitment.

4. When does a decision have to be made?

    If the decision must be made immediately, then you know that they have a strong need and also a strong interest in you. Stall at least until the next day to allow yourself some time to sleep on it before giving your answer. Be comfortable with your decision or don't do it.

5. How many people have already been presented?

   If a large number, than the odds are that the hiring company has a backup candidate that will made an offer if you refuse or delay your own decision on the offer.

6. What is the long term opportunity for someone taking the position offered?

   Again, if you're looking for future growth, you need to be comfortable with the answer to this question.

Topics you should not discuss with recruiters:

1. Your knowledge about job openings in your field, until you have found and accepted a job yourself. Don't create unwanted competition for yourself.

2. Whether you are using other recruiters.

   To do so would reduce their interest in working with you.

RECAP

If an executive search firm doesn't have the experience in your field or the placement industry, it isn't likely that this firm will be a source for your job search.

If they don't handle a large number or the right type of hiring companies or if they have an excessive number of job seekers on file, this firm may not a good choice for facilitating your job search.

Also, if they do not handle a large number of job openings, especially in your field, then chances are slim they will be of any meaningful help to you.

Remember, executive recruiters provide companies with a service first, supporting job seekers is secondary, so continue your job search elsewhere too.

INDEX CROSS REFERENCE BY SPECIALTY

**Specialty: A
(Advertising)**

AGRI-Associates
Agri-Tech Personnel Inc

**Specialty: B
(Banking)**

AGRI-Associates
Dunhill Search of Omaha Inc
Eggers Consulting Company Inc
Key Employment Services
Management Recruiters
    International
McGladrey & Pullen Search
    Group
R E B & Associates Inc
Robert Half International
Smith Bradley & Associates
The Human Resource Group

**Specialty: C
(Computers & Data Processing)**

AGRI-Associates
CompuSearch
CompuSearch of Overland Park
Eggers Consulting Company Inc
Key Employment Services
Management Recruiters
Management Recruiters
    International

McGladrey & Pullen Search
    Group
Morgan Hunter Corp
Personnel Search
Resource Placement Group III
Robert Half International
Search One Inc
The Career Connection

**Specialty: E
(Engineering)**

AGRI-Associates
Agri-Tech Personnel Inc
Best Personnel Service
City & National Employment
Crum & Associates
Dunhill Professional Search Inc
Eggers Consulting Company Inc
Executive * Engineering Search
Flaming & Associates
Gallagher & Brei Associates
Key Employment Services
Management Recruiters
    International
McGladrey & Pullen Search
    Group
Personnel Search
The Career Connection
The Human Resource Group
The Lincoln Group Inc

**Specialty: F
(Finance & Accounting)**

AGRI-Associates
Agri-Tech Personnel Inc
Bowman & Marshall
CompuSearch
Eggers Consulting Company Inc
Financial Careers
Key Employment Services
Management Recruiters
 International
McGladrey & Pullen Search
 Group
Morgan Hunter Corp
Noll Executive Search
Personnel Search
Robert Half International
Source Finance
The Career Connection

**Specialty: G
(General Applications)**

A T Kearney Executive Srch
Adams Inc
American Management
 Resources
Amerilink Ltd
Anne Jones Personnel
Apex Systems
Baehr David J & Assocs
Bellevue Personnel Resume
Bernhard Haldane Assocs
Best Personnel Service
Brinkman & Assoc
Bryant D F & Co

Cambridge Tempositions Inc
Career Transition Specialists
Careers Unlimited Inc
Continental Business Systems
Crippin Inc
Dunhill of Shawnee Mission
Dunhill Personnel of Fargo
Dunhill Professional Search
EFL Associates
Evergreen Information
Execu-Search International
Execusearch Inc
Executive Recruiters
Executive Resources Ltd
Express Service Temporary
Eyler Associates
Farha Placement Agency
Flaming & Associates
Francis & Associates
G E Smith Assoc
G R I
Gary Baer Associates
George Waterman Executive
Gleason & Associates
Image Builders Consulting
J B Bowers & Assoc Inc
J L Sage & Company
J Sherriff & Assoc
Jobnet
JR Associates
Koster & Kompany
MacArthur Church & Keres
Management Recruiters
Management Recruiters
 International
Management Recruiters-Liberal
Management Resource Group
Martin-Smith Personnel Svc

McDonald Sandi Associates
McGladrey & Pullen
McKirchy & Company Inc
Mid America Search
Network of Excellence Inc
O'Leary & Company
Personnel Incorporated
Personnel Management
    Resources
Peterson Group
Petrolink USA Inc
Professional Personnel Svc
Recruiters International Inc
Reed & Associates
Resume Experts Systems
Rose Leonetti & Assocs Inc
Shirley Michael Associates
Smith Brown & Jones
Snelling & Snelling Conslts
Spence Ewing & Assoc Inc
Spencer Reed & Associates
Staff Mid-America
Strategic Staff Management
The Lincoln Group Inc
Values Based Leadership
Waterman George Executive
    Search
Weinstein S E Company
Williams & Co
Winn Group
Wood-Glavin Inc
York & Company

Specialty: H
(Healthcare)

Bruce J Kelly & Associates Inc
Crum & Associates
Exec- U - Med Recruiters
Management Recruiters
    International
McGladrey & Pullen Search
    Group
Med Resources
Medical Search Institute
Personnel Search
Sherriff & Associates
Smith Bradley & Associates

Specialty: I
(Insurance)

Eggers Consulting Company Inc
Key Employment Services
Management Recruiters
    International
McGladrey & Pullen Search
    Group
Morgan Hunter Corp
The Garrison Organization

Specialty: M
(Manufacturing)

AGRI-Associates
Agri-Tech Personnel Inc
Best Personnel Service
Bowman & Marshall
City & National Employment

Dunhill Professional Search Inc
Executive * Engineering Search
Flaming & Associates
Harrison Moore Inc
Key Employment Services
Management Recruiters International
McGladrey & Pullen Search Group
Personnel Search
The Career Connection
The Lincoln Group Inc

Specialty: O
(Office Administration)

AGRI-Associates
Agri-Tech Personnel Inc
Morgan Hunter Corp
Noll Executive Search

Specialty: P
(Personnel/Human Resources)

AGRI-Associates
Agri-Tech Personnel Inc
Best Personnel Service
Management Recruiters International
McGladrey & Pullen Search Group

Specialty: R
(Research & Development)

AGRI-Associates
Agri-Tech Personnel Inc
Gallagher & Brei Associates
Management Recruiters International
The Lincoln Group Inc

Specialty: S
(Sales & Marketing)

Agra Placements Ltd
AGRI-Associates
Agri-Tech Personnel Inc
Crum & Associates
Dunhill Professional Search Inc
Execu-Search International
Key Employment Services
Management Recruiters International
McGladrey & Pullen Search Group
Noll Executive Search
Sales Consultants
Sales Search Intl

Specialty: T
(Travel, Food & Hospitality)

AGRI-Associates

Executive Recruiters

OTHER SPECIFIC SPECIALTIES:

Specialty: Agribusiness

Agra Placements Ltd
AGRI-Associates

Specialty: Agribusiness

Agra Placements Ltd
Agri-Tech Personnel Inc
Hedlin Ag Enterprises Inc
The Human Resource Group

Specialty: Automotive

William J Elam & Associates

Specialty: Credit Card

R E B & Associates Inc

Specialty: Construction

The Human Resource Group

Specialty: Consumer Packaged Goods

The Lincoln Group Inc

Specialty: Electronics

Tele-Electronics Co

Specialty: Environmental

Dunhill Search of Omaha Inc

Specialty: Food & Food Manufacturing

Agri-Tech Personnel Inc
The Lincoln Group Inc

Specialty: Foundry Industry

Harrison Moore Inc

Specialty: Horticulture

Agra Placements Ltd

Specialty: Management

City & National Employment
Crum & Associates
Smith Brown & Jones

Specialty: Packaging/Paper

Lunney Hadden & Associates

Specialty: Pharmaceutical

The Lincoln Group Inc
William J Elam & Associates

Specialty: Printing/Printing Ink

Lunney Hadden & Associates

Specialty: Production Machining

Harrison Moore Inc

Specialty: Retail

Crum & Associates

Specialty: Telecom

Tele-Electronics Co

Specialty: Therapist

Crum & Associates

Office Manager
A T Kearney Executive Srch
600 5th Ave Plz
Des Moines, IA 50309
(515) 245-4244
Specialty: G
Executive Search

Office Manager
Adams Inc
11404 W Dodge Road
Omaha, NE 68154
(402) 493-3301
Specialty: G
Executive Search

Gary Follmer, Manager
Agra Placements Ltd
4949 Pleasant Ste 1
West Des Moines, IA 50266-5494
(515) 225-6562
(515) 225-7733 FAX
Specialty: Agribusiness, Horticulture
Contingency/Retainer Search

Office Manager
Agra Placements Ltd
4949 Pleasant Street
West Des Moines, IA 50266
(515) 225-6562
Specialty: Agriculture,S, Management
Executive Search

Dale Unmisig
AGRI-Associates
109 South Center Street
Geneseo, IL 61254
(309) 944-8890
(309) 944-8891 FAX
Specialty: A,B,C,E,F,M,O,P,R,S,T (Agribusiness)
Contingency/Retainer Search

Dale Pickering, Pres
Agri-Tech Personnel Inc
3113 NE 69th Street
Kansas City, MO 64119
(816) 453-7200
(816) 453-6001 FAX
Specialty: A,E,F,M,O,P,R,S, Agriculture, Food Manufacturing
Contingency Executive Search

Office Manager
American Management Resources
3408 Woodland Ave Ste 401
West Des Moines, IA 50265
(515) 222-9044
Specialty: G
Executive Search

Office Manager
Amerilink Ltd
810 12 St NW
Mason City, IA 50401
(515) 424-8344
Specialty: G
Executive Search

Office Manager
Anne Jones Personnel
10965 Granada Ln
Shawnee Mission, KS 66211
(913) 491-3309
Specialty: G
Executive Search

Office Manager
Apex Systems
7593 Main Street
Ralston, NE 68127
(402) 592-5206
Specialty: G
Executive Search

Office Manager
Baehr David J & Assocs
6301 W 126th Terr
Shawnee Mission, KS 66209
(913) 491-4096
Specialty: G
Executive Search

Office Manager
Bellevue Personnel Resume
1820 Hillcrest Dr
Bellevue, NE 68005
(402) 291-6611
Specialty: G
Executive Search

Office Manager
Bernhard Haldane Assocs
121 Whittier St
Wichita, KS 67207
(316) 689-6868
Specialty: G
Executive Search

Louis Kram, Pres
Best Personnel Service
8901 Stateline Ste 242
Kansas City, MO 64114
(816) 361-3100
(816) 361-0861 FAX
Specialty: E,G,M,P
Contingency Executive Search

Office Manager
Bowman & Marshall
P O Box 25503
Overland Park, KS 66225
(913) 648-3332
(913) 341-9596 FAX
Specialty: F,M
Contingency/Retainer Search

Office Manager
Brinkman & Assoc
733 S National Ave
Fort Scott, KS 66701
(316) 223-5637
Specialty: G
Executive Search

Brian M Kelly, Sr Consultant
Bruce J Kelly & Associates Inc
9300 Metcalf Ave Ste 920
Overland Park, KS 66212
(913) 648-6832
(913) 648-3836 FAX
Specialty: H (Physicians & Surgeons)
Contingency/Retainer Search

Office Manager
Bryant D F & Co
7600 W 110th
Shawnee Mission, KS 66210
(913) 345-2806
Specialty: G
Executive Search

Office Manager
Cambridge Tempositions Inc
400 S Clinton St #208
Iowa City, IA 52240
(319) 354-8281
Specialty: G
Executive Search

Office Manager
Career Transition Specialists
10550 Barkley St
Shawnee Mission, KS 66212
(913) 383-9192
Specialty: G
Executive Search

Bud Burris, Pres
Careers Unlimited Inc
5001 College Blvd
Leawood, KS 66211
(913) 469-1709
(913) 469-5568 FAX
Specialty: G
Contingency/Retainer Search

Michael C Grillo, Manager
City & National Employment
221 E 4th Street
P O Box 267
Waterloo, IA 50704
(319) 232-6641
(319) 232-5700 FAX
Specialty: E,M (Management)
Contingency/Retainer Search

Office Manager
Compu Search
S Alpine Centre Penthouse
Bettendorf, IA 52722
(319) 359-3503
Specialty: C
Executive Search

Jean Felton, Admin Manger
CompuSearch
210 Gateway Ste 434
Lincoln, NE 68505
(402) 467-5549
Specialty: C,F
Contingency/Retainer Search

Office Manager
CompuSearch of Overland Park
9401 Indian Creek Pky
Shawnee Mission, KS 66210
(913) 661-9400
Specialty: C
Executive Search

Office Manager
Continental Business Systems
5845 Horton St
Shawnee Mission, KS 66202
(913) 677-0200
Specialty: G
Executive Search

Office Manager
Crippin Inc
5100 W 95th St
Shawnee Mission, KS 66207
(913) 381-1288
Specialty: G
Executive Search

Rose Crum, Owner
Crum & Associates
4001 Center Street Ste 218
Omaha, NE 68105
(800) 243-3613
(402) 344-4380 FAX
Specialty: E,H,S,Management, Retail,Therapist
Contingency/Retainer Search

Office Manager
Dunhill of Shawnee Mission
7101 College Blvd Ste 120
Shawnee Mission, KS 66210
(913) 451-8333
Specialty: G
Executive Search

Office Manager
Dunhill Personnel of Fargo
109 1/2 Broadway St N
Fargo, ND 58102
(701) 235-3719
Specialty: G
Executive Search

Office Manager
Dunhill Professional Search
7500 Main St
Ralston, NE 68127
(402) 331-1644
Specialty: G
Executive Search

Office Manager
Dunhill Professional Search
9718 Rosehill Rd
Shawnee Mission, KS 66215
(913) 599-6270
Specialty: G
Executive Search

Charles F Dummer, Pres
Dunhill Professional Search Inc
1007 2nd Avenue
Kearney, NE 68847-7305
(308) 234-4555
(308) 234-4556 FAX
Specialty: E,M,S,**(Outdoor Power Equipment Exclusively)**
Contingency Executive Search

Ken Jasperson CPC, Owner
Dunhill Search of Omaha Inc
P O Box 37287
Omaha, NE 68137
(402) 334-1233
(402) 334-0290 FAX
Specialty: B,Environmental
Contingency Executive Search

Office Manager
EFL Associates
7101 College Blvd Ste 550
Overland Park, KS 66210-1891
(913) 451-8866
Specialty: G
Executive Search

Office Manager
Eggers Consulting Company Inc
11272 Elm Street
Omaha, NB 68144-4788
(402) 333-3480
Specialty: B,C,E,F,I
Executive Search

Office Manager
Evergreen Information
P O Box 704
Fairfield, IA 52556
(515) 472-9626
Specialty: G
Executive Search

Paul Martin, Pres
Exec- U - Med Recruiters
221 East 4th Street
P O Box 267
Waterloo, IA 50704
(319) 232-6641
(319) 232-5700 FAX
Specialty: H (Physician,Medical)
Contingency/Retainer Search

Harold Metzinger, Managing Principal
Execu-Search International
1999 N Amidon Street Ste 100
Wichita,KS 67203
(316) 838-1199
Specialty: G,S
Contingency/Retainer Search

Office Manager
Execusearch Inc
8101 College Blvd
Overland Park, KS 66210
(816) 561-8650
Specialty: G
Executive Search

Gary Warner
Executive * Engineering Search
1119 Linden Lane
Mt Pleasant, IA 52641
(319) 986-5254
Specialty: E,M
Contingency/Retainer Search

Office Manager
Executive Recruiters
6608 Goode Dr
Shawnee Mission, KS 66216
(913) 962-2478
Specialty: G
Executive Search

Office Manager
Executive Resources Ltd
3716 Ingersoll Ave Ste B
Des Moines, IA 50312
(515) 287-6880
Specialty: G
Executive Search

Office Manager
Express Service Temporary
6031 S 58th St Ste C
Lincoln, NE 68516
(402) 421-2100
Specialty: G
Executive Search

Office Manager
Eyler Associates
400 Locust Street Ste 170
Des Moines, IA 50309
(515) 245-4244
Specialty: G
Executive Search

Office Manager
Farha Placement Agency
2535 N Wilderness Ct
Wichita, KS 67226
(316) 681-3334
(316) 681-3337 Fax
Specialty: G
Executive Search

Office Manager
Financial Careers
6405 Metcalf Ave
Shawnee Mission, KS 66202
(913) 262-8635
Specialty: F
Executive Search

Peter Flaming, Pres
Flaming & Associates
120 W 6th St Ste 120
Newton, KS 67114
(316) 283-3851
(316) 283-3859 FAX
Specialty: E,G,M
Contingency Executive Search

N Kay Francis
Francis & Associates
6923 Vista Drive
West Des Moines, IA 50266
(515) 221-9800
Specialty: G
Retained Executive Search

Office Manager
G E Smith Assoc
10100 Santa Fe Dr
Shawnee Mission, KS 66212
(913) 341-9116
Specialty: G
Executive Search

Office Manager
G R I
R R 1
Fairfield, IA 52556
(515) 472-6005
Specialty: G
Executive Search

Randall Brei, Sr Consultant
Gallagher & Brei Associates
2598 28th Avenue
Marion, IA 52302
(319) 377-9196
(319) 377-9219 FAX
Specialty: E,R(Electronics & Software)
Contingency Executive Search

Donald G Gallagher, Sr Consultant
Gallagher & Brei Associates
1145 Linn Ridge Road
Mount Vernon, IA 52314
(319) 895-6455
Specialty: E,R(Electronics & Software)
Contingency Executive Search

Office Manager
Gary Baer Associates
P O Box 446
Fairfield, IA 52556
(515) 472-8589
Specialty: G
Executive Search

Office Manager
George Waterman Executive
11879 W 112th St
Shawnee Mission, KS 66210
(913) 451-4448
Specialty: G
Executive Search

Office Manager
Gleason & Associates
8208 Melrose Drive Ste 210
Pine Ridge II
Lenexa, KS 66214
(913) 381-0040
Specialty: G
Retained Executive Search

Jim Hicks, Recruiter
Harrison Moore Inc
7638 Pierce Street
Omaha, NE 68124
(402) 391-5494
(402) 391-5381 FAX
Specialty: M,Foundry Industry,
Production Machining
Contingency/Retainer Search

Office Manager
J L Sage & Company
907 E Jefferson Ave
Fairfield, IA 52556
(515) 472-3003
Specialty: G
Executive Search

Lawrence K Hedlin
Hedlin Ag Enterprises Inc
1025 Ashworth Road
West Des Moines, IA 50265
(515) 223-1408
Specialty: Agriculture
Executive Search

Office Manager
J Sherriff & Assoc
9332 W 116th Ter
Shawnee Mission, KS 66210
(913) 451-2112
Specialty: G
Executive Search

Office Manager
Image Builders Consulting
133 Main Ave W
West Fargo, ND 58078
(701) 277-1650
Specialty: G
Executive Search

Office Manager
Jobnet
109 1/2 Broadway St N
Fargo, ND 58102
(701) 237-9262
Specialty: G
Executive Search

Office Manager
J B Bowers & Assoc Inc
9332 W 116th Ter
Shawnee Mission, KS 66210
(913) 451-9191
Specialty: G
Executive Search

Office Manager
JR Associates
2912 Western Ave
Davenport, IA 52803
(319) 424-1680
Specialty: G
Executive Search

Dennis Leiminger, General Mgr
Key Employment Services
1001 Office Park Road Ste 320
West Des Moines, IA 50265-2567
(515) 224-0446
(515) 224-6599 FAX
Specialty: B,C,E,F,I,M,S
Executive Search

Office Manager
Koster & Kompany
7700 University Ave #A
Des Moines, IA 50325
(515) 255-4311
Specialty: G
Executive Search

Richard Lunney, Pres
Lunney Hadden & Associates
P O Box 7790
Overland Park, KS 66207-0790
(913) 648-5142
(913) 648-5157 FAX
Specialty: Printing, Printing Ink, Paper, Packaging
Contingency/Retainer Search

Office Manager
MacArthur Church & Keres
9802 Nicholas Street
Omaha, NE 68114
(402) 393-2197
Specialty: G
Executive Search

Cheryl Plagge, Manager
Management Recruiters
1312 4th SW Ste 102
Mason City, IA 50401
(515) 424-1680
(515) 424-6868 FAX
Specialty: C
Contingency Executive Search

Office Manager
Management Recruiters
7171 Mercy Rd
Omaha, NE 68106
(402) 397-8320
Specialty: G
Executive Search

Office Manager
Management Recruiters
9401 Indian Creek Pkwy
Shawnee Mission, KS 66210
(913) 661-9300
Specialty: G
Executive Search

Office Manager
Management Recruiters
3261 University Ave Ste D
Waterloo, IA 50701
(319) 236-1510
Specialty: G
Executive Search

Jean Felton, Admin Manager
Management Recruiters International
210 Gateway Ste 434
Lincoln, NE 68505
(402) 467-5534
Specialty: B,C,E,F,G,H,I,M,P,R,S,
Contingency/Retainer Search

Office Manager
Management Recruiters Intl
10 E Cambridge Circle Dr
Suite 190
Kansas City, KS 66103
(913) 342-1316
Specialty: G
Executive Search

Office Manager
Management Recruiters-Liberal
322 N Lincoln Ave
Liberal, KS 67901
(316) 626-5085
Specialty: G
Executive Search

Office Manager
Management Resource Group
400 Main St
Davenport, IA 52801
(319) 323-3333
Specialty: G
Executive Search

Office Manager
Management Resource Group
400 Main Street
Davenport, IA 52801
(319) 323-3333
Specialty: G
Executive Search

Office Manager
Martin-Smith Personnel Svc
100 E 9th St
Lawrence, KS 66044
(913) 842-1515
Specialty: G
Executive Search

Office Manager
McDonald Sandi Associates
716 S 153 Avenue Circle
Omaha, NE 68144
(402) 334-2881
Specialty: G
Executive Search

Office Manager
McGladrey & Pullen
221 3 Avenue SE
Cedar Rapids, IA 52401
(712) 365-8900
Specialty: G
Executive Search

Thomas Hamilton, Principal
McGladrey & Pullen Search Group
400 Locust Ste 640
Des Moines, IA 50309
(515) 281-9200
(515) 284-1545 FAX
Specialty: B,C,E,F,H,I,M,P,S
Retainer ONLY Executive Search

Office Manager
McKirchy & Company Inc
P O Box 825
Bettendorf, IA 52722
(319) 332-8888
Specialty: G
Executive Search

Office Manager
Med Resources
8105 W 99th St
Shawnee Mission, KS 66212
(913) 648-6064
Specialty: H
Executive Search

Office Manager
Medical Search Institute
11111 W 95th St
Shawnee Mission, KS 66214
(913) 541-4040
Specialty: H
Executive Search

Office Manager
Mid America Search
4401 Westown Pky Ste 226
West Des Moines, IA 50265
(515) 225-1942
Specialty: G
Executive Search

Jerry Hellebusch, Owner
Morgan Hunter Corp
6800 College Blvd Ste 550
Overland Park, KS 66211
(913) 491-3434
Specialty: C,F,I,O
Contingency/Retainer Search

Office Manager
Network of Excellence Inc
10816 W 123rd
Shawnee Mission, KS 66213
(913) 897-2177
Specialty: G
Executive Search

Office Manager
Noll Executive Search
2120 S 72nd Street Ste 900
Omaha, NE 68124
(402) 391-7736
Specialty: F,O,S
Executive Search

Mike O'Leary
O'Leary & Company
509 Black Bldg
Fargo, ND 58102
(701) 235-2404
Specialty: G
Executive Search

Office Manager
Peterson Group
8700 Monrovia St
Shawnee Mission, KS 66215
(913) 599-4804
Specialty: G
Executive Search

Office Manager
Personnel Incorporated
516 Equitable Building
Des Moines, IA 50309
(515) 243-7687
Specialty: G
Executive Search

Office Manager
Petrolink USA Inc
11915 Birch
Shawnee Mission, KS 66209
(913) 338-1111
Specialty: G
Executive Search

Office Manager
Personnel Management Resources
3200 SW Belle Ave
Topeka, KS 66614
(913) 273-9332
Specialty: G
Executive Search

Office Manager
Professional Personnel Svc
3201 Pioneers Blvd Ste 222
Lincoln, NE 68502
(402) 483-7821
Specialty: G
Executive Search

Jacky Woody CPC CIPC, Mgr
Personnel Search
8744 Frederick St
Omaha, NE 68124
(402) 397-2980
(402) 397-1122 FAX
Specialty: C,E,F,H,M
Contingency/Retainer Search

Ray Brixius, Pres
R E B & Associates Inc
256 N 115 Street Ste 7B
Omaha, NE 68154
(402) 333-8248
(402) 333-0372 FAX
Specialty: B(Banking & Credit Card)
Contingency/Retainer Search

Office Manager
Recruiters International Inc
11330 Q St Ste 218
Omaha, NE 68137
(402) 339-9839
Specialty: G
Executive Search

Office Manager
Reed & Associates
1200 Valley West Drive
West Des Moines, IA 50266
(515) 226-8893
Specialty: G
Executive Search

Gaylord Hrubes, Manager
Resource Placement Group III
221 East 4th Street
P O Box 267
Waterloo, IA 50704
(319) 232-6641
(319) 232-5700 FAX
Specialty: C(AS/400,PC,IBM Main Frame)
Contingency/Retainer Search

Office Manager
Resume Experts Systems
10500 Barkley St Ste 225
Shawnee Mission, KS 66212
(913) 381-4484
Specialty: G
Executive Search

Office Manager
Robert Half International
317 6th Ave Ste 700
Des Moines, IA 50309
(515) 244-4414
Specialty: B,C,F
Executive Search

Office Manager
Rose Leonetti & Assocs Inc
600 5th Ave Plz
Des Moines, IA 50309
(515) 282-3232
Specialty: G
Executive Search

Office Manager
Sales Consultants
200 1st Ave NE Ste 203
Cedar Rapids, IA 52401
(319) 365-8900
Specialty: S
Executive Search

Office Manager
Sales Search Intl
513 N Mesquite St
Olathe, KS 66061
(913) 829-2197
Specialty: S
Executive Search

Larry W Halley, Owner
Search One Inc
10800 Farley St Ste 320
Overland Park, KS 66210
(913) 451-2408
(913) 451-0274 FAX
Specialty: C(AS/400)
Contingency Executive Search

Don Smith, Pres
Smith Brown & Jones
800 W 47th Ste 510
Kansas City, MO 64112
(816) 531-4770
(816) 531-5010 FAX
Specialty: G,Middle,High Level Management
Executive Search

Julie Sherriff, Pres
Sherriff & Associates
10983 Granada Lane Ste 202
Overland Park, KS 66211
(913) 451-2112
Specialty: H(Physicians)
Contingency/Retainer Search

Office Manager
Snelling & Snelling Conslts
609 1/2 1st Ave N
Fargo, ND 58102
(701) 237-0600
Specialty: G
Executive Search

Office Manager
Shirley Michael Associates
7015 College Blvd
Shawnee Mission, KS 66211
(913) 491-0240
Specialty: G
Executive Search

Office Manager
Source Finance
10300 W 103rd Street Ste 101
Overland Park, KS 66214
(913) 888-3054
Specialty: F
Executive Search

Office Manager
Smith Bradley & Associates
Box 25094 Corporate Woods
Overland Park, KS 66225
(913) 345-2531
Specialty: B,H
Executive Search

Office Manager
Spence Ewing & Assoc Inc
218 6th Ave Ste 420
Des Moines, IA 50309
(515) 283-2473
Specialty: G
Executive Search

Executive Recruiters 165

Office Manager
Spencer Reed & Associates
10999 Metcalf Ave
Shawnee Mission, KS 66210
(913) 345-9898
Specialty: G
Executive Search

Office Manager
Staff Mid-America
7602 Pacific St Ste 100
Omaha, NE 68114
(402) 391-2065
Specialty: G
Executive Search

Office Manager
Strategic Staff Management
202 S 71 St
Omaha, NE 68157
(402) 393-5226
Specialty: G
Personnel Consultant/Recruiter

Office Manager
Tele-Electronics Co
204 Farm Credit Bldg
Omaha, NE 68114
(402) 346-3421
Specialty: Telecom,Electronics
Executive Search

Twila F Deahl, Owner
The Career Connection
1621 S University Drive Ste 215
Fargo, ND 58103
(701) 232-4614
(701) 241-9822 FAX
Specialty: C,E,F,M
Contingency/Retainer Search

Office Manager
The Garrison Organization
600 5th Avenue Plaza
Des Moines, IA 50309
(515) 245-4240
Specialty: I
Executive Search

Will Canine, Pres
The Human Resource Group
808 Fifth Avenue
Des Moines, IA 50309-1315
(515) 243-8855
(515) 243-8866 FAX
Specialty: B,E,Agriculture,
Construction
Contingency/Retainer Search

Jack Mosow, Pres
The Lincoln Group Inc
100 N 56th Ste 416
P O Box 5208
Lincoln, NE 68505
(402) 434-5919
(402) 434-5915 FAX
Specialty: E,G,M,R,Consumer
Packaged Goods,Pharmaceutical,
Food
Contingency Executive Search

Office Manager
Values Based Leadership
1716 S 153 Av Cir
Omaha, NE 68144
(402) 333-2648
Specialty: G
Executive Search

Office Manager
Waterman George Executive Search
11879 W 112th St
Shawnee Mission, KS 66210
(913) 451-3016
Specialty: G
Executive Search

Office Manager
Weinstein S E Company
1830 2nd Ave Suite 240
Rock Island, IL 61201
(309) 794-1992
Specialty: G
Executive Search

Office Manager
William J Elam & Associates
210 Gateway Mall Ste 434
Lincoln, NE 68505-2438
(402) 467-5638
Specialty: Automotive, Pharmaceutical
Executive Search

Office Manager
Williams & Co
814 Pierce St
Sioux City, IA 51101
(712) 252-4041
Specialty: G
Executive Search

Office Manager
Winn Group
501 Lawrence Ave
Lawrence, KS 66049
(913) 842-7111
Specialty: G
Executive Search

Jim Glavin
Wood-Glavin Inc
8695 College Blvd Ste 260
Overland Park, KS 66210
(913) 451-2015
Specialty: G
Retained Executive Search

Office Manager
York & Company
203 E Burlington Ave Ste 1
Fairfield, IA 52556
(515) 472-7127
Specialty: G
Executive Search

EXECUTIVE SEARCH BONUS SECTION

SELECTED RECRUITERS FROM OUR NATIONAL DATABASE

The following pages contain the specialty cross-reference listings to an alphabetical list of active executive search firms from our national data base.

The alphabetical listing is immediately after the cross-reference list.

INDEX CROSS REFERENCE BY SPECIALTY

Specialty: A
(Advertising)

Able Personnel Inc
Affluence International
Armstrong-Hamilton Assoc
Atlanta Arts Agency Inc
Bristol Assoc Inc
Leonard Corwen Co
Parsons Anderson & Gee
Recruiting Resources Group

Specialty: B
(Banking)

Able Personnel Inc
APA International Placement Consultants
Armstrong-Hamilton Assoc
Badger Group The
Chartwell Partners International
COR Management Services Ltd
Corporate Search Partners Inc
Cubbage & Associates
Fogec Consultants
Kling Personnel
Profile Financial Search
Recruiting Resources Group
Santangelo Consultants Inc
Weterrings & Agnew Inc

Specialty: C
(Computers & Data Processing)

Abacus Consultants
APA International Placement Consultants
Badger Group The
Carlson Bentley Associates
Chartwell Partners International
Commonwealth Consultants
Comptime Inc
CompuPro Inc
COR Management Services Ltd
Corporate Search Partners Inc
Daly Consulting & Search
Dunhill Professional Search
Executive Recruiters
Frankel & Adams
Harris Personnel Resources
J Gross & Assoc
J Q Turner and Assoc Inc
Mark Nine Systems Inc
Parsons Anderson & Gee
Peter W Ambler Company
Recruiting Resources Group
Rigel Computer Resources
Santangelo Consultants Inc
Source EDP
Systems Research Group
Weterrings & Agnew Inc

**Specialty: E
(Engineering)**

Able Personnel Inc
Akin Trombly Associates
Armstrong-Hamilton Assoc
Ashway Ltd Agency
Badger Group The
Bartlett Bunn & Travis
Corporate Search Partners Inc
Cubbage & Associates
Executive Recruiters
First Choice Search
Frankel & Adams
Harris Personnel Resources
Health Industry Consultants Inc
J Gross & Assoc
J Q Turner and Assoc Inc
John R Stephens & Associates
Lasky & Co
Marvin L Silcott
McKee Company The
Med Quest Associates Div
Noah Associates
Parsons Anderson & Gee
Peter W Ambler Company
Professional Recruiting Offices
Recruiting Resources Group
Rigel Computer Resources
Roth Young Personnel
Santangelo Consultants Inc
Systems Research Group
Weterrings & Agnew Inc

**Specialty: F
(Finance & Accounting)**

Able Personnel Inc
Accountants Executive Search
Akin Trombly Associates
APA International Placement
   Consultants
Armstrong-Hamilton Assoc
Badger Group The
Bankers Group
Berger & Associates
Chartwell Partners International
CompuPro Inc
COR Management Services Ltd
Corporate Search Partners Inc
Cubbage & Associates
Ellis & Associates Inc
Executive Recruiters
Fogec Consultants
I S C of Atlanta Inc
Lee & Burgess Associates
Leonard Corwen Co
Marvin L Silcott
Noah Associates
Parsons Anderson & Gee
Paull Norsell & Assoc Inc
Peter W Ambler Company
Profile Financial Search
Recruiting Resources Group
The Foster McKay Group
Tower Associates Inc
Weterrings & Agnew Inc

**Specialty: G
(General Applications)**

A H Justice & Assoc
Able Personnel Inc
Badger Group The
Barrington Associates Ltd
Blue Garni & Company
Conley Associates Inc
Corporate Search Partners Inc
Cubbage & Associates
DHR International Inc
Ellis & Associates Inc
Ford Payton & Davis
Goodrich & Sherwood Co
Health Industry Consultants Inc
Katherine C Patterson Consulting
Kristan Associates Executive Search
Lamalie Amrop International
Noah Associates
Omni Executive Recruiters
Paul R Ray & Company Inc
Paull Norsell & Assoc Inc
Peter W Ambler Company
Santangelo Consultants Inc
Sigma Group International
The Employment Assistance Group
Thomas Graig Associates

Specialty: H
(Healthcare)

Able Personnel Inc
Bartlett Bunn & Travis
Bristol Assoc Inc
Charles Bernard & Associates Inc
Dunhill Personnel of Aurora
Executive Referral Service

Fogec Consultants
Health Industry Consultants Inc
I S C of Atlanta Inc
Peter W Ambler Company
Professional Recruiting Offices
Roth Young Personnel

Specialty: I
(Insurance)

Affluence International
Armstrong-Hamilton Assoc
Ashway Ltd Agency
Bartlett Bunn & Travis
Bridgers Goetlz & Associates
Ellis & Associates Inc
Fogec Consultants
Lee & Burgess Associates
Professional Recruiting Offices
Profile Financial Search
Recruiting Resources Group
Roth Young Personnel

Specialty: L
(Legal)

APA International Placement Consultants
Armstrong-Hamilton Assoc
Bartlett Bunn & Travis
Chartwell Partners International
Corporate Search Partners Inc
Ellis & Associates Inc
Marvin L Silcott
The Howard C Bloom Co

Specialty: M
(Manufacturing)

A H Justice & Assoc
Akin Trombly Associates
Ashway Ltd Agency
Badger Group The
Bristol Assoc Inc
Charles Bernard & Associates Inc
Corporate Search Partners Inc
Cubbage & Associates
Evie Kreisler & Assoc
Executive Recruiters
Executive Referral Service
First Choice Search
Fogec Consultants
Frankel & Adams
Harris Personnel Resources
Health Industry Consultants Inc
I S C of Atlanta Inc
J Gross & Assoc
J Q Turner and Assoc Inc
Kristan Associates Executive Search
Lasky & Co
Lee & Burgess Associates
Marvin L Silcott
McKee Company The
Noah Associates
Parsons Anderson & Gee
Paull Norsell & Assoc Inc
Peter W Ambler Company
Profile Financial Search
Roth Young Personnel
Santangelo Consultants Inc
Systems Research Group
Weterrings & Agnew Inc

Specialty: O
(Office Administration)

Able Personnel Inc
Affluence International
APA International Placement Consultants
Armstrong-Hamilton Assoc
Corporate Search Partners Inc
Ellis & Associates Inc
Health Industry Consultants Inc
Noah Associates
Parsons Anderson & Gee
Recruiting Resources Group
Roth Young Personnel

Specialty: P
(Personnel/Human Resources)

Able Personnel Inc
Armstrong-Hamilton Assoc
Badger Group The
CompuPro Inc
Corporate Search Partners Inc
Executive Recruiters
Fogec Consultants
Frankel & Adams
Harris Personnel Resources
Leonard Corwen Co
Noah Associates
Parsons Anderson & Gee
Peter W Ambler Company
Recruiting Resources Group
Roth Young Personnel
Weterrings & Agnew Inc

**Specialty: R
(Research & Development)**

Akin Trombly Associates
Ashway Ltd Agency
Badger Group The
COR Management Services Ltd
First Choice Search
Health Industry Consultants Inc
J Q Turner and Assoc Inc
Lasky & Co
Marvin L Silcott
Noah Associates
Parsons Anderson & Gee
Paull Norsell & Assoc Inc
Peter W Ambler Company
Professional Recruiting Offices
Weterrings & Agnew Inc

**Specialty: S
(Sales & Marketing)**

Able Personnel Inc
Akin Trombly Associates
Armstrong-Hamilton Assoc
Badger Group The
Bartlett Bunn & Travis
Bob Maddox Associates
Charles Bernard & Associates Inc
Commonwealth Consultants
CompuPro Inc
Corporate Search Group The
Corporate Search Partners Inc
Cubbage & Associates
Executive Recruiters
Frankel & Adams
Harris Personnel Resources

Health Industry Consultants Inc
I S C of Atlanta Inc
Kristan Associates Executive Search
Leonard Corwen Co
MarketSearch Inc
McKee Company The
Med Quest Associates Div
Noah Associates
Parsons Anderson & Gee
Paull Norsell & Assoc Inc
Peter W Ambler Company
Recruiting Resources Group
Rigel Computer Resources
Roth Young Personnel
Systems Research Group
Weterrings & Agnew Inc

**Specialty: T
(Travel, Food & Hospitality)**

Bristol Assoc Inc
Coast To Coast Executive Search
Cubbage & Associates
Executive Referral Service
J Gross & Assoc
Roth Young Personnel
William-Johns Company

OTHER SPECIFIC SPECIALTIES:

Specialty: Bearings

A H Justice & Assoc

Executive Recruiters

Specialty: Bilingual

APA International Placement Consultants

Specialty: Bio Tech/Genetic Engineering

Marvin L Silcott

Specialty: Bio-medical

Health Industry Consultants Inc

Specialty: Bio-Tech

Fortune Personnel Consultants
Health Industry Consultants Inc

Specialty: Building Products

Kristan Associates Executive Search

Specialty: Communications

Leonard Corwen Co

Specialty: Construction

John R Stephens & Associates

Specialty: Consumer Products

Evie Kreisler & Assoc

Specialty: Direct Marketing

Executive Careers

Specialty: Electronics

Dunhill Professional Search
ESP III Consulting Services

Specialty: Energy

Marvin L Silcott

Specialty: Environmental

Lee & Burgess Associates
Marvin L Silcott

Specialty: Food Industry

SBB & Associates

Specialty: Hazardous Waste

Adams Group The

Specialty: Hi-Tech

J Gross & Assoc
McKee Company The

Specialty: Laboratory Management

Adams Group The

Specialty: Management/ Management Consulting

Fischer Management Consultants
J Gross & Assoc
Santangelo Consultants Inc

Specialty: Meat Industry

Mahoney & Assoc Ltd

Specialty: Medical Devices

Dunhill Professional Search

Specialty: Mining

Omni Executive Recruiters

Specialty: Not For Profit

Executive Careers

Specialty: Office Furniture

Kristan Associates Executive Search

Specialty: Pharmaceutials

Executive Referral Service
Fortune Personnel Consultants

Specialty: Primary Metal

A H Justice & Assoc

Specialty: Publishing

Able Personnel Inc

Specialty: Pulp & Paper

John R Stephens & Associates

Specialty: Real Estate

Chartwell Partners International

Specialty: Retail

Evie Kreisler & Assoc
Executive Careers
Executive Referral Service

Specialty: Science & Technology

Ashway Ltd Agency

Specialty: Supermarket & Grocery Wholesalers

Supermarket Search Group

Specialty: Technology

Dunhill Professional Search

Specialty: Telecom

ESP III Consulting Services

Specialty: Transportation

A H Justice & Assoc

Specialty: Women & Minorities

J Gross & Assoc

Jack King, Pres
A H Justice & Assoc
P O Box 58345
Houston, TX 77258
(713) 474-7700
(713) 474-9382 FAX
Specialty: G,M,Primary Metal, Transportation,Bearings
Contingency/Retainer Search

Stephen J Kukoy, Pres
Abacus Consultants
1777 S Harrison Street Ste 404
Denver, CO 80210
(303) 759-5064
(303) 759-9846 FAX
Specialty: C
Contingency/Retainer Search
Since 1976

Dan Gardner, VP
Able Personnel Inc
280 Madison Avenue Ste 807
New York, NY 10016
(212) 689-5500
Specialty: A,B,E,F,G,H,O,P,S, Publishing
Contingency/Retainer Search

Julie Weiss, Branch Mgr
Accountants
Executive Search
200 N LaSalle
Chicago, IL 60601
(312) 782-7711
Specialty: F
Executive Search

B W Adams, Pres
Adams Group The
7840 Madison Ave Ste 185
Fair Oaks, CA 95628
(916) 966-5050
(916) 966-7070 FAX
Specialty: Exclusively Hazardous Waste, Laboratory Management
Contingency/Retainer

David Wolfe, Exec. Dir.
Affluence International
8855 Atlanta Ave, Ste 356
Huntington Beach, CA 92646
(714) 753-3313
Specialty: A,I,O
Contingency/Retainer

Dale Unmisig
AGRI-Associates
109 South Center Street
Geneseo, IL 61254
(309) 944-8890
(309) 944-8891 FAX
Specialty: A,B,C,E,F,M,O,P,R,S,T (Agribusiness)
Contingency/Retainer Search

Duane Trombly, Principal
Akin Trombly Associates
9974 Scripps Ranch Blvd, Ste 150
San Diego, CA 92123
(619) 453-7880
(619) 453-7880 FAX
Specialty: E,F,M,R,S
Executive Search

Raisa Katz
APA International Placement Consultants
551 Fifth Avenue Ste 322
New York, NY 10017
(212) 490-3798
(212) 687-8384 FAX
Specialty: B,C,F,L,O,Bilingual
Contingency/Retainer Search

Glenda Peters
Armstrong-Hamilton Assoc
203 N La Salle St, Ste 2100
Chicago, IL 60601
(312) 558-1461
(312) 915-0848 FAX
Specialty: A,B,E,F,I,L,O,P,S
Recruiting Firm

Steven King, Pres
Ashway Ltd Agency
295 Madison Avenue
New York, NY 10017
(212) 679-3300
(212) 447-0583 FAX
Specialty: E,R,I,M,Science & Technology
Contingency/Retainer Search

Caroline Amory, Pres
Atlanta Arts Agency Inc
475 Rock Springs Road NE
Atlanta, GA 30324
(404) 873-0850
(404) 874-6684 FAX
Specialty: A
Executive Search

Fred Badger, Pres
Badger Group The
4125 Blackhawk Plaza Cir Ste 270
Danville, CA 94506
(415) 736-5553
(415) 736-5554 FAX
Specialty: B,C,E,F,G,M,P,R,S
Retainer Only

David Umlauf
Bankers Group
10 S Riverside Plaza, Ste 1424
Chicago, IL 60606
(312) 930-9456
Specialty: F
Retained

Keith Tallis, Pres
Barrington Associates Ltd
3949 Holcomb Bridge Rd
Ste 202
Norcross, GA 30092
(404) 447-0200
Specialty: G
Retained Executive Search

Ed Bunn, Managing Partner
Bartlett Bunn & Travis
6320 LBJ Freeway Ste 224
Dallas, TX 75240
(214) 980-0950
(214) 980-0160 FAX
Specialty: E,H,I,L,S
Contingency/Retainer Search

Alan H Berger, Owner
Berger & Associates
One Sansome St Ste 2100
San Francisco, CA 94104
(415) 951-4750
Specialty: F
Executive Search

Patricia Blue, Partner
Blue Garni & Company
1505 Bridgeway Ste 103
Sausalito, CA 94965
(415) 332-1110
(415) 332-1131 FAX
Specialty: G
Executive Search

Robert E Maddox, Pres
Bob Maddox Associates
3390 Peachtree Rd NE Ste 1102
Atlanta, GA 30326
(404) 231-0558
(404) 231-0558 FAX
Specialty: S,Sales Management
Executive Search

Norman J Goeltz
Bridgers Goetlz & Associates
4725 Peachtree Corners Cir
Ste 195
Norcross, GA 30092
(404) 368-9835
(404) 447-1220 FAX
Specialty: I
Executive Recruiter

James J Bright Jr, Pres
Bristol Assoc Inc
5777 W Century Bl #705
Los Angeles, CA 90045
(310) 670-0525
(310) 670-4075 FAX
Specialty: A(Direct Marketing),H,M(Food),T
Executive Recruiter

Donald E Miller, Pres
Carlson Bentley Associates
3889 Promontory Court
Boulder, CO 80304
(303) 443-6500
(303) 443-6500 FAX
Specialty: C
Contingency/Retainer Search

Charles B Courtois, CEO
Charles Bernard & Associates Inc
3951 Snapfinger Pkwy Ste 540
Decatur, GA 30035
(404) 284-2666
(404) 284-8318 FAX
Specialty: H,M,S
Retainer Only
Executive Search

David deWilde, Managing Dir
Chartwell Partners International
275 Battery St Ste 2180
San Francisco, CA 94111-3305
(415) 296-0600
(415) 296-7588 FAX
Specialty: B,C,F,L,Real Estate, Mortgage Banking
Executive Search

Dennis Updyke, Principal
Coast To Coast Executive Search
3000 Pearl Street Ste G-2
Boulder, CO 80301
(303) 449-5922
(303) 443-9484 FAX
Specialty: T(Hospitality)
Contingency/Retainer Search

David Aiken, Pres
Commonwealth Consultants
4840 Roswell Rd NW Ste C-302
Atlanta, GA 30342
(404) 256-0000
(404) 256-3625 FAX
Specialty: C,S
Executive Recruiter

John O'Keefe, Owner
Comptime Inc
3420 Executive Center Drive
Ste 114
Austin, TX 78731
(512) 343-1171
(512) 343-0142 FAX
Specialty: C
Contingency Executive Search

Douglas J Baniqued, Principal
CompuPro Inc
162 N Franklin, Ste 602
Chicago, IL 60606
(312) 263-5507
(312) 263-4237 FAX
Specialty: C,F,P,S
Executive Search

Gordon Housfeld, Pres
Conley Associates Inc
31191 W Beaver Lake Rd
Hartland, WI 53029
(414) 367-7300
Specialty: G
Retainer Only Senior
Executive Search

Matthew Grove, Research
Assistant
COR Management Services Ltd
420 Lexington Avenue
New York, NY 10017
(212) 599-2640
(212) 599-3048 FAX
Specialty: B,C,F,R
Contingency Executive Search

Bruce Moore, Principal
Corporate Search Group The
3555 Timmons Lane Ste 1000
Houston, TX 77027
(713) 893-1719
(713) 622-5184
Specialty: S
Contingency/Retainer Search

John Horn, Pres
Corporate Search Partners Inc
1050 Walnut Street Ste 212
Boulder, CO 80302
(303) 444-3678
(303) 440-1416 FAX
Specialty: B(Mortgage Banking),
E,F,G,L, M,O,P,S
Contingency/Retainer Search

Durinda Scheider, Office Mgr
Cubbage & Associates
3590 Shiloh Rd NW Ste B-202
Kennesaw, GA 30144
(404) 424-6361
Specialty: B,E,F,G,M,S,T
Executive Search

Mike Daly, Owner
Daly Consulting & Search
1615 Bonanza, Ste 313
Walnut Creek, CA 94596
(510) 256-0393
(510) 256-9733 FAX
Specialty: C
Data Processing All Levels
Executive Recruiter

Jeff J Dandurand, VP
DHR International Inc
5215 N O'Connor Blvd Ste 200
Irving, TX 75062
(214) 556-1051
Specialty: G
Executive Search

Sandra Funt, VP
Dunhill Personnel of Aurora
P O Box 260085
Highland Ranch, CO 80126-0085
(303) 721-0525
(303) 721-0747 FAX
Specialty: H, Medical
Contingency/Retainer Search

Julie Raab, Dir Tech Grp
Dunhill Professional Search
9 Executive Circle Ste 240
Irvine, CA 92714
(714) 474-6666
(714) 474-6674 FAX
Specialty C, Technology,
Electronics, Medical Devices
Executive Search

Joe Ellis, Principal
Ellis & Associates Inc
1250 Capital of TX Hwy S
Building 3 Ste 620
Austin, TX 78746
(512) 328-5067
(512) 328-5069 FAX
Specialty: F,G,I,L,O
Executive Search

L L Areaux CPC, Pres
ESP III Consulting Services
433 E Las Colinas Blvd Ste 940
Irving, TX 75039
(214) 869-0837
(817) 575-4597 (Fax Call)
Specialty: Electronics/Telecom
Retainer Only Executive Search

Debbi Kreisler, EVP
Evie Kreisler & Assoc
2575 Peachtree Rd NE Ste 24C
Atlanta, GA 30305
(404) 262-0599
(404) 262-0699 FAX
Specialty: M,Retail,
Consumer Products
Executive Search

Annette R Segil, Pres
Executive Careers
1801 Ave of the Stars #640
Los Angeles, CA 90067
(310) 306-0360
(310) 578-7524 FAX
Specialty: Retail, Direct Marketing,Not For Profit
Contingency/Retainer Search

Jerry Taylor, Manager
Executive Recruiters
P O Box 1766
Bellevue, WA 98009
(206) 447-7404
(206-447-7428 FAX
Specialty: C,E,F,M,P,S
Executive Search

Bruce Freier, Pres
Executive Referral Service
8745 W Higgins Rd, Ste 470
Chicago, IL 60631
(312) 693-6622
(312) 693-8466 FAX
Specialty: H,M,T Retail, Pharmaceutical
Executive Recruiter

Michele J Hale, Mgr
First Choice Search
3515 SW Alaska
Seattle, WA 98126
(206) 938-1944
(206) 937-5245 FAX
Specialty: E,M,R
Contingency & Retainer
Executive Search

Norman T Fischer, Pres
Fischer Management Consultants
380 Madison Avenue 7th Floor
New York, NY 10017
(212) 737-3400
(212) 986-5669 FAX
Specialty: Executive/Senior Management ONLY
Contingency/Retainer Search

Thomas G Fogec
Fogec Consultants
400 N Executive Dr Ste 455
Brookfield, WI 53005
(414) 789-2747
(414) 785-4184 FAX
Specialty: B,F,H,I,M,P
Executive Search

Leo Cacciotti, Pres
Ford Payton & Davis
900 Wilshire Bl #1240
Los Angeles, CA 90017
(213) 624-1297
Spccialty: G
Executive Search

Marc Kasten, Pres
Fortune Personnel Consultants
5300 W Centruy Bl #208
Los Angeles, CA 90045
(310) 410-9662
(310) 410-0606 FAX
Specialty: Medical Devices, Biotech, Pharmaceutials
Executive Recruiter

Howard Frankel, VP
Frankel & Adams
8834 Prichett Dr
Houston, TX 77096-2628
(713) 666-1001
(713) 666-1001 (Touch 33) FAX
Specialty: C,E,M,P,S
Contingency/Retainer Search

Andrew Sherwood, Chairman
Goodrich & Sherwood Co
521 5th Avenue Floor 27
New York, New York 10175-0060
(212) 697-4131
Specialty: G
Retainer ONLY Executive Search

Vera E Harris CPC, Owner
Harris Personnel Resources
2201 N Collins Ste 260
Arlington, TX 76011
(817) 265-9190
(817) 543-3155 FAX
Specialty: C,E,M,P,S
Contingency/Retainer Recruiter

Jon K Fitzgerald, Pres
Health Industry Consultants Inc
9250 East Costilla Ave Ste 600
Englewood, CO 80112
(303) 790-2009
(303) 790-2021 FAX
Specialty: E,G,H,M,O,R,S
Bio-medical,Bio-tech
Retained Only Executive Search

A Arthur Kwapisz, Pres
I S C of Atlanta Inc
300 Interstate N Pkwy Ste 330
Atlanta, GA 30339
(404) 952-2340
(404) 952-2071 FAX
Specialty: F,H,M,S
Executive Recruiter

Jerry Gross, Partner
J Gross & Assoc
2722 Fircrest Ct
Stafford, TX 77477
(713) 261-5236 (Also Fax)
Specialty: C,E,M,T,General
Management,Hi-Tech,
Women & Minorities
Contingency/Retainer Search

Jim Turner, Pres
J Q Turner and Assoc Inc
3140 S Peoria Street Ste K-200
Aurora, CO 80014-3155
(303) 671-0800
Specialty: C,E,M,R
Contingency/Retainer Search

John R Stephens, Pres
John R Stephens & Associates
7007 Gulf Frwy Ste 202
Houston, TX 77087
(713) 644-0067
(713) 644-4332 FAX
Specialty: E,Construction,
Pulp & Paper
Contingency/Retainer Search

Executive Recruiters 183

Katherine C Patteron, Owner
Katherine C Patterson Consulting
476 Jackson St Ste 200
San Francisco, CA 94111
(415) 398-2622
Specialty: G
Executive Search

Len Adams CPC
Kling Personnel
180 Broadway Ste 501
New York, NY 10038
(212) 964-3640
(212) 964-6959 FAX
Specialty: B
Contingency/Retainer Search

Office Manager
Kristan Associates Executive Search
12 Greenway Plaza Ste 1100
Houston, TX 77046
(713) 961-3040
(713) 961-3626 FAX
Specialty: G,S,M,Office Furnishings,Building Products
Retainer Only Executive Search

Anthony B Cashen, Managing Partner
Lamalie Amrop International
489 Fifth Ave Ste 1400
New York, NY 10017
(212) 953-7900
(212) 953-7907 FAX
Specialty: G
Retainer ONLY Executive Search

Sid Lasky, Owner
Lasky & Co
6334 Gaston Ave Ste 214
Dallas, TX 75214
(214) 826-8450
(214) 826-1628 FAX
Specialty: E,M,R
Contingency/Retainer Search

Ed Ryer, VP
Lee & Burgess Associates
9110 E Nichols Avenue Ste 128
Englewood, CO 80112
(303) 799-0044
(303) 799-4404 FAX
Specialty: F,I,M,Environmental
Retained Executive Search

Len Corwen, Pres
Leonard Corwen Co
P O Box 350453
Brooklyn, NY 11235
(718) 646-7581
Specialty: A,F,P,S, Communications
Contingency/Retainer Search

Charles F Mahoney
Mahoney & Assoc Ltd
6065 Roswell Rd ME Ste 1355
Atlanta, GA 30328
(404) 457-5501
Specialty: Meat Industry
Contingeny Executive Search

Martha Harris, Office Manager
Mark Nine Systems Inc
333 N Glenoaks Bl #675
Burbank, CA 91502
(310) 849-5874
(310) 841-6402 FAX
Specialty: C
Since 1978

Linda Barkwell, Pres
MarketSearch Inc
216 N Green Bay Rd Ste 111
Thiensville, WI 53092
(414) 242-9103
(414) 242-7945 FAX
Specialty: S
Executive Search

Marvin L Silcott, Pres
Marvin L Silcott & Assoc Inc
7557 Rambler Rd Ste 1336
Dallas, TX 75231
(214) 369-7802
(214) 369-7875 FAX
Specialty: E,F,L,M,R,Bio Tech/Genetic Engineering, Energy,Evironmental
Retainer Only Executive Search

Ed McKee
McKee Company The
404 Pharr Rd Ste A-205
Atlanta, GA 30305
(404) 261-9029
Specialty: E,M,S,Hi-Tech
Executive Search Since 1983

Judy Stiles, Director
Med Quest Associates Div
9250 E Costilla Avenue Ste 600
Englewood, CO 80112
(303) 790-2009
(303) 790-2021 FAX
Specialty: E,S,(Medical Devices)
Contingency Executive Search

Norman Houle, Pres
Noah Associates
P O Box 606
Amawalk, NY 10501
(914) 737-1819
(914) 737-1853 FAX
Specialty: E,F,G,M,O,P,R,S
Contingency/Retainer Search

E C "Bud" Nott, Pres
Omni Executive Recruiters
559 E Pikes Peak Avenue Ste 320
Colorado Springs, CO 80903
(719) 578-1828
Specialty: G, Mining
Contingency Executive Search

Arthur J Fandel, Assoc Recruiter
Parsons Anderson & Gee
500 Kreag Road
Pittsford, NY 14534
(716) 586-8679
(716) 248-2996 FAX
Specialty: A,C,E,F,M,O,P,R,S
Contingency/Retainer Search

Executive Recruiters

David B Radden, Gen Mgr
Paul R Ray & Company Inc
2029 Century Park E #1000
Los Angeles, CA 90067
(213) 557-2828
(213) 277-0674 FAX
Specialty: G
Executive Search

Paul E Norsell, Pres
Paull Norsell & Assoc Inc
P O Box 6686
Auburn, CA 95604-6686
(916) 269-0121
(915) 268-3202 FAX
Specialty: F,G,M,R,S
Senior Exex On National Basis
Salary $100K +
Executive Search

Peter W Ambler, Owner
Peter W Ambler Company
14643 Dallas Pkwy Ste 537
Dallas, TX 75240
(214) 404-8712
(214) 404-8761 FAX
Specialty: C,E,F,G,H,M,P,R,S
Retainer Only Executive Search

Erwin J. Schneekluth, CEO
Professional Recruiting Offices
4250 Executive Square, Ste 440
La Jolla, CA 92037
(619) 587-1313
(619) 587-2090 FAX
Specialty: E,H,I,R
Executive Search

Joseph Lagattula, Owner
Profile Financial Search
55 W Wacker Dr, Ste 400
Chicago, IL 60601
(312) 641-0555
Specialty: B,F,I,M
Executive Search

Glenda Peters, VP
Recruiting Resources Group
25 E Wacker Dr, Ste 2700
Chicago, IL 60601
(312) 836-1200
Specialty: A,B,C,E,F,I,O,P,S
Executive Search

Rita Aslley, Pres
Rigel Computer Resources
1611 116th Ave NE Ste 226
Bellevue, WA 98004
(206) 646-4990
(206) 646-3058 FAX
Specialty: C,E,S(Hi-Tech)
Executive Search

Collen S Rinehardt, Pres
Roth Young Personnel
9725 E Hampden Avenue Ste 300
Denver, CO 80231
(303) 755-0075
(303) 743-0877 FAX
Specialty: E,H,I,M,P,O,S,T
Contingency Executive Search

Richard Santangelo,
Managing Partner
Santangelo Consultants Inc
60 East 42nd Street
New York, NY 10165
(212) 867-6664
Specialty: B,C,E,H,M,
Management Consulting
Contingency/Retainer Search

Mark Barlow, Pres
SBB & Associates
3330 Gwinnett Plantation Way NW
Duluth, GA 30136
(404) 476-5120
Specialty: Food Industry
All Disciplines
Contingency Executive Search

George L Reisinger, Pres
Sigma Group International
717 17th Street Ste 1440
Denver, CO 80202-3314
(303) 292-6720
Specialty: G
Executive Search

Mike Varrichio, Mgr Dir
Source EDP
6606 L B J Frwy Ste 148
Dallas, TX 75240
(214) 387-1600
(214) 387-0204 FAX
Specialty: C,
Contingency/Retainer Search

Stephen Godlewski, Pres
Supermarket Search Group
P O Box 9215
Downers Grove, IL 60151
(708) 960-9980
(708) 960-9041 FAX
Specialty: Supermarket &
Grocery Wholesalers
Executive Search

Stephen Gebler, Pres
Systems Research Group
5962 La Place Ct Ste 160
Carlsbad, CA 92008
(619) 438-7333
(619) 438-8673 FAX
Specialty: C,E,M,S (Computer Systems)
Executive Search

Warren Samuel CPC, Pres
The Employment Assistance Grp
17610 Midway Road 134 LB307
Dallas, TX 75287
(214) 407-0474
(214) 931-8374 FAX
Specialty: G
Retainer Only Executive Search

Keith Roberts, VP
The Foster McKay Group
535 Fifth Avenue 32nd Floor
New York, NY 10017
(212) 867-5780
(212) 808-9039 FAX
Specialty: F
Executive Search

Howard Bloom, Pres
The Howard C Bloom Co
5000 Quorum Drive Ste 160
Dallas, TX 75240
(214) 385-6455
(214) 385-1006 FAX
Specialty: L
Executive Search

Bill Kresich, Pres
William-Johns Company
14081 Yorba Ste 202
Tustin CA 92680
(714) 544-1222
(714) 544-6555 FAX
Specialty: T
Contingency/Retainer Search

Michael Schiaffo
Thomas Graig Associates
P O Box 33
Massapeqah Park, NY 11762
(516) 798-8200
(516) 798-8696 FAX
Specialty: G
Executive Search

Donna Weeden, VP
Tower Associates Inc
1099 18th Street Ste 2020
Denver, CO 80202
(303) 292-3650
(303) 298-0110 FAX
Specialty: F(Primary Focus CPAs)
Contingency Executive Search

Thomas Quinn, Partner
Weterrings & Agnew Inc
1200 Midtown Tower
Rochester, NY 14604
(716) 454-3888
(716) 454-5998 FAX
Specialty: B,C,E,F,M,P,R,S
Employment Agency/Recruiter

JOB SEEKERS SURVIVAL HINTS

The old saying that the early bird gets the worm certainly applies to the task of job hunting.

Stay ahead of the pack by doing the following:

- Review Sunday's paper as soon as it is out on the news stands. Check for any new job openings for which you are qualified and respond the same day by mail with a tailored cover letter and resume.

- Call the first thing Monday morning on all offers with a phone number to announce your interest and to let the employer know that a resume is on its way. Work to qualify the job offer and create an interest on their behalf. If the employer appears interested, then try to set up a time for an interview.

- Get the morning paper each day and send your responses out by noon on any new job openings.

- Maintain a log of all ads responded to so that you have a record of the cover letter sent, date/time of the ad, source of the ad, and the date/time of your response. Cross reference this log to new job openings to prevent a duplication of effort on your part.

PLAINS STATES
JOB SEEKERS SOURCEBOOK

Section 6

Database/Network/Referral Services

Overview

Database/Network/Referral services provide another viable avenue for candidates to follow in the course of their job search.

These services are often free or provided for a nominal fee. Using these referral/networking services provides the job seeker with the advantage of a much expanded exposure to the available job market.

Utilization of database services is usually a **passive** activity until an interview is requested by a hiring company that has obtained access to your record and indicates an interest.

Use of these services should be done only to supplement other job search activities such as responding to specific newspaper ads, personal networking, using employment agencies or executive recruiters, or other employment services.

The value of any of these types of services to a job seeker depends upon several things:

- the quality and cost of the service,
- the kind of job being sought and your experience,
- the access or exposure that these services have to hiring companies.

Useful information on how to select and use a quality database, network, or referral service has been provided on the next few pages.

How to Select a Database, Network or Referral Service

Selecting a database/referral service to help you find a job or change jobs requires careful research on your part.

To avoid unnecessary expense, completing this research is a must! To increase the chances of obtaining a job through this approach means that you must qualify and then select only services that you wish to represent you in your job search. To assist you in this process we've outlined some important selection criteria that should be useful.

Selection Criteria:

The selection of the right database service to support your job search efforts should be based upon a combination of the following criteria:

Specialty — Does the database service specialize in serving job seekers and hiring companies in your career field?

If so, the service will be useful in your job search. If they deal exclusively in your discipline, so much the better.

Experience — How long has the database service been in business?

It is best to select a service that has been around at least one year. These services will already have established a network of contacts with hiring companies and will be better sources for job openings.

Referrals	Was this service referred to you by someone else in your field?

If so, then a referral will give you a better idea of the quality and type of service being offered. |
| Location | Is the service regional? And if so, where?

If so, then your exposure to the local job market may be much better by using a local regional database. However, if you are looking for a job away from where you live, then the answer to this question will allow you to focus your efforts on other services which provide either national databases or strong databases in other geographic areas. |
| Quality | Does this service have a good reputation and do they present themselves in a professional manner?

The best way to determine this is to talk to other job seekers and to check with the Better Business Bureau. If you're unhappy with what you see or find, keep looking. |
| Cost | Is the cost of this service within reason, considering the type of service being offered?

If yes, then the chances are better that participation in the service will give you broader exposure to a larger share of the employment market. |

Questions to ask to qualify a Database/Network/Referral Service:

1. How long have they been in business?

    The longer a firm has been in the business, the more contacts they are likely to have, therefore the odds of their being able to help you are better.

2. How many client companies are they working with?

    The more client companies that use the database or referral service, the greater your opportunity of finding a job.

3. How easy is it for companies to use?

    Avoid those services that are difficult for companies to use, as chances are many of the companies being served aren't actively using the service.

4. How many people are being placed using their service?

    If they can't tell you or the number appears extremely low, then the odds are that this service isn't worth the money.

5. How long will your entry remain on file?

    If it is just for a short period of time, consider the renewal cost when comparing one service to another.

    Also a good service will allow you to request that your entry be removed once you have found a new position.

6. How easy is it for you to use?

   A good database or referral service should be relatively easy for you to use. More importantly, the service should provide the flexibility to accommodate your specific job experiences in a meaningful manner.

7. What does the service cost for you to use?

   Identify all of the costs associated with the use of the service. Measure the value of the service, by finding out how many companies are actively using the service. Divide this number into your cost to determine the your opportunity cost.

Using a Database, Network or Referral Service

To maximize your opportunity of using a database or referral service to reach an employer in search of someone with your skills, you need to follow a few important rules.

RULE 1. Employers perform specific searches to fill their job orders.

Therefore, do everything possible to help make their job easier. This includes being as specific as possible about all of your job skills and work history.

RULE 2. Employers searching a database see as many as a hundred entries per day.

This means that you must get noticed and stay noticed by them to be considered for a job opening. This is best done by being creative yet clear in your explanation of your work history.

RULE 3. Employers know their business, but they don't know you or how well you can perform your job.

This means that they need your help in getting to know you. Remember, you know your job history and performance record best, so tell them what you are good at.

Describe and identify the important features of previous accomplishments.

Furnish them with a means of measuring performance, such as a list of awards or reference letters.

RULE 4. Two thirds of all job hunters spend five hours or less a week on their job search.

Spend **full-time** on your job search, at least 30 hours a week.

If the service doesn't handle the right type of hiring companies or doesn't show a large number of placements, then it may be not be best for you.

The most significant point to remember, is that database and referral services are passive approaches for seeking a job.

There is no guarantee that anyone will search the database and come up with your entry as a match.

<u>Therefore, it is very important that you continue to use other active approaches to further your job search.</u>

Sarah Morgan Taylor
Access/Networking in the Public Interest
96 Mt Auburn St
Cambridge, MA 02140
(617) 495-2178
Database of college graduates and job openings
Database Service

Office Manager
AIA Referral Network
American Institute of Architects
1735 New York Ave NW
Washington, DC 20006
Available to AIA members and student members. Job Seekers can call for position search and receive a print out of positions. Call/write for fee and format
Job Service

Office Manager
Air Transportation Association Resume Bank
1709 New York Ave, NW
Washington, DC 20006-5206
No phone Number available
Free resume forwarding service for airline industry employees
Referral Service

Office Manager
American Association of Advertising Agencies
666 Third Avenue 13th Floor
New York, NY 10017-4565
(212) 682-2500
Placement Service and Minority Internship Program

Roger Miller, Pres
American Association of Finance & Accounting
5757 Wilshire Blvd Ste 447
Los Angeles, CA 90056
(213) 852-1311
Resume Database Service for Accounting & Financial
Resume Database

Office Manager
American Federation of Police
1000 Connecticut Ave NW Ste 9
Washington, DC 20036
Specialty: Referral Service
Organization of Government & Private Law Enforcement Officers

Office Manager
American Institute of Biological Sciences (AIBS)
730 11th Street NW
Washington, DC 20001-4584
Speciality: Offers Placement Services & Maintains Computerized Job Lists. Call or write for details
Professsional Association

Office Manager
American Theatre Association
1010 Wisconsin Ave NW
6th Floor
Washington, DC 20007
(202) 342-7530
Speciality: Offers placement assistance call or write for specifics
Professional Association

Office Manager
American Public Health Association
1015 15th Street NW
Washington, DC 20005
Office Manager
Speciality: H Placement Services Available call or write for details
Professional Organization

Office Manager
Artists in Print
665 3rd
San Francisco, CA 94107
(415) 243-8244
Specialty: Job Referral for Graphic Artists
Referral Service

James C Rodgers
American Society of Design Engineers
P O Box 931
Arlington Heights, IL 60006
Speciality: E Job Referrals available write for specifics
Professional Association

Office Manager
Association for Direction Instruction
P O Box 10252
Eugene, OR 97440
(503) 485-1293
Speciality: Association of public school and special education teachers and university instructors. Offers placement services. Call/for specifics.
Professional Association

Office Manager
**Aviation Maintenance
Foundation International**
P O Box 2826
Redmond, WA 98073
(206) 828-3917
(206) 827-6895 FAX
Speciality: Aviation Maintenance Industry Placement Services available call/write for details
Trade Association

Colin Hanna
Bank Executives Network
300 S High St
West Chester, PA 19382
(215) 431-1900
Database service to banks of active job seekers
Database Service

Office Manager
BPI - Business People Inc
33 S 6th St Ste 2985
Minneapolis, MN 55402
(612) 370-0550
(612) 344-1648 FAX
Provides regional job fairs; Offers resume mailing service for those unable to attend a job fair. Resumes sent to hiring companies fair for $20.
Job Fairs/Mailing Service

Harry Allcock, Mgr
Career Placement Registry Inc
302 Swann Ave
Alexandria, VA 22301
(703) 683-1085
(703) 683-0246 FAX
Resume Database, $45 for six months activation
Database Service

Lloyd Bach, Mgr
**Christian Employment
Opportunity Network**
164 N Gary Ave
Carol Stream, IL 60188
No Phone available
A grapevine of Chicago churches attempting to link the unemployed underemployed with hiring companies. Free
Referral Service

Office Manager
**Club Managers Association
of America**
1733 King Street
Alexandria, VA 22314
(703) 739-9500
(703) 739-0124 FAX
Specialty: Placement Service & Executive Career Service Committee
Association of Managers

Office Manager
College Media Advisors
MJ-300
Department of Journalism
Memphis State University
Memphis, TN 38152
(901) 678-2401
Speciality: Professional Assoc serving advisors,directors,college students etc interested in college & university student media. Offers placement referrals Call or write for specifics.
Professional Association

Michael L Harp, Pres
Confidential Christian Connections
1767 Benningfield Dr Ste 1125-N
Marietta, GA 30064-9870
(404) 590-0340
Specialty: Christian Ministry Postions (Ministers,Education, Administrative,etc)
Database/Referral Service

Office Manager
CORS
One Pierce Place, Ste 300 East
Itasca, IL 60143
(708) 250-8677
(800) 323-1352
Database of job seekers for Employers Job Search Service
Candidate Finder Service

Office Manager
CU Career Connection
University of Colorado
Campus Box 133
Boulder, CO 80309-0133
(303) 492-4127
Hot line of social services job openings. $20/two months for an access code. Touchtone phone required to key code, field of interest & geographic area.
Job Service

Office Manager
Datamation Databank
265 S Main St
Akron, OH 44308
(216) 762-0279
Electronic Database, matches job with your qualifications, Free
Database Service

Office Manager
Dial-A-Job
National Association of Interpretation
P O Box 1892
Ft Collins, CO 80522
Call (303) 491-7410 24 hours-for recording of full time, temporary & seasonal jobs in environment, education, interpretation, etc. Updated weekly.
Job Service

Office Manager
Electronic Industries Association
1722 I Street NW Ste 300
Washington, DC 20006
(202) 457-4900
Specialty: Placement Service
Trade Organization

Office Manager
Employers' Jobnet
PO Box 325
Readstown, WI 54652
(608) 629-57499
Electronic Database of Job Openings
Database Service

Mary Ellen Kite, Sales Rep
Employment Network Inc
5299 Roswell Rd Ste 102
Atlanta, GA 30342
(404) 303-8818
(404) 303-9016 FAX
Specialty: Job Opportunities via a computerized job bank. Need a service agreement to access. There is a cost for this agreement, call for details
Networking Company

Office Manager
Executive Telecom System Inc
1000 Waterway Blvd
Indianapolis, IN 46202
(317) 633-2045
Resumes of active job seekers, obtained thru CareerPro offices
$35 for 24 weeks activation
Database Service for employers

Office Manager
Federal Job Matching Service
Breakthrough Publications
P O Box 594
Millwood, NJ 10546
$30.00 fee to match your education/experience to federal job requirement and return a list. You need special questionnaire/ turnaround time about 3 weeks. Call for specifics
Job Service

Bob Mikesell, Mgr
First Interview
5500 Interstate N Parkway
River Edge One, Ste 425
Atlanta, GA 30328
(404) 952-1058
Database service to contingency employment agencies specializing in sales/marketing
Database Service

Office Manager
Foreign & Domestic Teachers Bureau
Box 1063
Vancouver, WA 97666
Clearing House For Teacher Job Placements

Mike Novak, Mgr
Graduating Engineers Employment Registry
Career Technologies Corp
138 Old River Rd
Andover, MA 01810
(508) 683-0098
Database service to companies interested in hiring engineers
Database Service

Office Manager
Health Personnel Options Traveling Service
2221 University Ave SE Ste 140
Minneapolis, MN 55414
Speciality: Health professionals (excludes physicians) are placed short term (4-26 weeks). No charge to candidates. Need special forms call for info.
Job Service

John Hawkins, Mgr
HRIN - College Recruitement Database-Executive Telecom System Inc
9585 Valparaiso Ct
Indianapolis, IN 46268
(317) 872-2045
Recent college grads resumes offered to hiring companies via Human Resources Info Network
Database Service

Brad Davis, Director
ICN
8855 Atlanta Ave, Ste 356
Huntington Beach, CA 92646
(714) 753-3312
Exchanges resumes on a referral basis within their network
Referral Service

Kenneth P Jeranek, Mgr
Insurance National Search
Kinsale-KPJ Consilum
68 W Main St
Oyster Bay, NY 11771
(516) 922-9450
Database of job seekers in the insurance industry
Database Service

Dr Frank L Greenagel
Inter Digital
25 Water Street
Lebanon, NJ 08833
(908) 832-2463
(908) 832-6081 FAX
Specialty: Computer Based Guide for Seeking Employment. Company offers software- "Looking for Work" with six modules designed to organize the job search and help identify resources. Call for Details
Software Firm

Office Manager
Job Mart
National Water Well Association
6375 Riverside Dr
Dublin, OH 43017
(614) 761-3222
Speciality: Job Seekers complete resume forms/blind ad. Ads are circulated to employers who may pay a fee to see the full resume. Cost to jobseeker is $20/12 months. Positions include geologists/scientists/engineers.
Job Service

Office Manager
Interior Design Educators Council
14252 Culver Drive Ste A-311
Irvine, CA 92714
(714) 551-1622
Specialty: Placement/ Recruitment Committee Council of Design Educators

Office Manager
Job NAA
Newspaper Association Job Bank
11600 Sunrise Valley Dr
Reston, VA 22091
(703) 648-1072
(800) 562-2672
Speciality: Newspaper Postions. 24 hour national job bank.
Job Service

Mike Conway, Sr Mgr
J O B S of Tampa Bay
One North Dale Mabry Ste 950
Tampa, FL 33609
(813) 876-2112
(813) 876-9599
Specialty: G
Referral Service

Office Manager
Job Referral Service
National Contract Managers Association
1912 Woodford Rd
Vienna, VA 22182
(800) 344-8096
(703) 448-9231
Speciality: Contract Manager, free service. Submit form with ten copies of your resume. Resumes on file for 6 months. Call for details.
Job Service

Office Manager
JobFest
800 Lee St
Des Plaines, IL
(708) 824-3378
Conducts Job Fairs
Job Fair Coordinator

Office Manager
Jobline BIOSOS
2100 Arch Street
Philadelphia, PA 19103-1399
(215) 587-4800
(800) 523-4806
(215) 587-2016 FAX
Speciality: On Line Database of Employment Opportunities in life sciences disciplines including academic, government & industry
Database Service

William W Griffin, Pres
JOBS
Alpha Systems, Inc
1510 Oakfield Ln
Roswell, GA
(404) 992-8663
Specialty: C,E,F,M,R,S, Distribution, Communications, General & Operations Mgt
Candidates are available for on-line search by job title, education, state, and salary. Call for details
Electronic Bulletin Board

Dwayne Miller, Mgr
JOBSource
Computerized Employment Systems
418 S Howes, Ste D
Ft Collins, CO 80521
(303) 493-1779
Database software for placement firms

Office Manager
kiNexus
640 N LaSalle St, Ste 560
Chicago, IL 60610
(800) 828-0422
(312) 642-0616 FAX
Resume Database Service for College Graduates, Free
Database Service

Office Manager
National Association of
Black Accountants
900 Second Street NE Ste 205
Washington, DC 20002
(202) 682-0222
(202) 682-33322 FAX
Speciality: F Offers placement service call or write for specifics
Professional Association

Office Manager
National Banking Network
2628 Barrett St
Virginia Beach, VA 23452
No telephone Number
Database service to contingency employment agencies specializing in banking
Database Service

Dr Ethel O Washington
National Association of Black Americans in Vocational Education (NAABAVE)
5057 Woodward Room 976
Detroit, MI 48202
(313) 494-1660
Speciality: Vocational Education Placement Service available call or write for specifics
Professional Association

Office Manager
National Employment Network
PO Box 7169
Alexandria, VA 22307
No telephone Number
Database service to hiring companies
Database Service

Office Manager
National Association of Black Women Attorneys
3711 MaComb Street NW
Washington, DC 20016
(202) 966-9393
Speciality: L Publishes Job Annoucements and is a job placement resource call or write for information
Professional Association

Mary Ann Weber, Pres
National Insurance Recruiters Association
Shiloh Careers
PO Box 831
Brentwood, TN 37024-0831
(615) 373-3090
Database of job seekers in the insurance industry
Database Service

Database/Network Referral Services

Dr Steve Johnson
National Resume Bank
Job Coach
901 E Grove St
Bloomington, IL 61701
(309) 829-3931
Resume database, 3 month listing free to job seekers. Free access to employers. Developed by the Professional Association of Resume Writers
Database Service

Thomas Murray, Pres
On-Line Personnel Services
1930 W Peoria Avenue Ste 405
Phoenix, AZ 85029
(602) 331-8220
(602) 331-8135 FAX
Specialty: G
Database Service

Office Manager
National Teachers Clearinghouse
P O Box 1257
Boston, MA 02188-1257
(617) 267-3204
Once registered you will receive reports of openings that match your experience. Fees $25-$100. Call for Specifics.
Job Service

Sharon Strong, Coordinator
Older Worker Employment
124 W 46th Street
Kearney, NE 68847
(308) 234-1851
(308) 234-1853 FAX
Specialty: Job Search Referral Consultant South Central NE Area Agency On Aging

Office Manager
Nationwide Interchange Service
PO Box 21390
Canton, OH 44701-1390
(216) 455-1433
Private industry database of active job seekers, available to placement firms only. See your personal recruiter.
Database Service

Office Manager
Paralegal Placement Network
P O Box 710
Solebury, PA 19009
(215) 938-1182
(215) 297-8697
Speciality: L, Job Matching. $15 registration fee for two years. Call for form and specifics.
Job Service

Bill Aberman, Chairman
Personnel Strategies
1809 So Plymouth Road
350 Ameribank Building
Minneapolis, MN 55305
Job Fairs

Office Manager
**Presort Association
of Government Accountants**
2200 Mt Vernon Ave
Alexandria, VA 22301
(703) 684-6931
Pay by the minute database of
500+ accountants, finance jobs.
$1.95 first minute $.95 thereafter.
Job Service

Paul Servass, Mgr
Printers Resume Network
Curtis Publishing Co
1000 Waterway Blvd
Indianapolis, IN 46202
(317) 636-1000
Database of job seekers
from the printing industry
Database Service

Office Manager
**Professional Resume File
National Research Council
Personnel Office**
2101 Constitution Ave NW
Washington, DC 20418
Free Service. Research Field
Send a copy of your resume and
ask that it be placed in this
file.
Job Service

Tom Robinson, Mgr
Pronet
University Pronet
Bowman Alumni House
Stanford University
Stanford, CA 94305
(415) 723-7569
Database of available
college graduates
Database Service

Office Manager
**Public Relations Society of
America**
33 Irving Place 3rd Floor
New York, NY 10003
(212) 995-2230
(212) 995-0757 FAX
Specialty: Job Referral Service
Professional Society

Database/Network Referral Services

Office Manager
Resume-Link
P O Box 218
Hillard, OH 43026
(800) 622-5441
Database of College Graduates
Database Service

Office Manager
Society of Certified Credit Executives
P O Box 27357
St Louis, MO 63141
(314) 991-3030
Speciality: Organization of credit executives certified through the organization's program. Offers placement services call or write or details
Referral Service

Office Manager
Softsource
527 James St
Geneva, IL 60134
(708) 879-1009
(708) 879-0807 FAX
Critique resume, select companies matching your background, send out letters for $2 per letter
Referral Service

Office Manager
Sole Electronic Job Referral Service
Society of Logistics Engineers
8100 Professional Pl Ste 211
New Carrollton, MD 20785
(800) 695-7653
(301) 459-8446
Free Service. Use your computer to connect to a national bulletin board of job listings.
Job Service

Office Manager
Special Libraries Association
1700 18th Street NW
Washington, DC 20009
(202) 234-4700
(202) 265-9317
Specialty: Resume Referral Service. Employment Clearing House At Annual Conference Association of Information Professionals In Special Libraries

Office Manager
Talent Bank
Trans Century Corporation
1724 Kalorama Rd NW
Washington, DC 20009
Free Service. Refers resumes to international employers. Must obtain their form to submit your resume.
Job Service

D J Baniqued
Techmatch
162 N Franklin Ste 602
Chicago, IL 60606
(312) 263-5507
(312) 263-4237 FAX
Database services
for: C,F,P,S
Database Service

Eric Sandberg, Sr VP
Texas S & L League
408 W 14th St
Austin, TX 78701
(512) 476-6131
Electronic Database of
job seekers in Banking or
Savings & Loan Industry
Database Service

Office Manager
U S Employment Opportunities-Banking/Finance
Washington Research Associates
2103 Lincoln Street
Arlington, VA 22207
(703) 276-8260
Speciality: On Line data base of current openings in banking & finance. Call or write for details
Database Service

Office Manager
Women In Information Processing
Lock Box 39173
Washington, DC 20016
(202) 328-6161
Specialty: Organization of women in computer, office automation,robotics/telecom. Offers resume bank,career counseling and resume help. Call or write for details.
Referral Service

Office Manager
Women In Sales Association
Eight Madison Avenue
P O Box M
Valhalla, NY 10595
(914) 946-3802
Specialty: Career Guidance Workshops. Referral Service Organization of Professional Saleswomen and Students

Tom Laughon, Pres
Your Employment Connection
8744 Landmark Road
Richmond, VA 23228
(804) 266-7344
(804) 266-7362 FAX
Specialty: A,S
Job Referral/Database Service

Susan R Kelly, Program Director
YWCA Career Assistance Network
225 SW 12th Street
Topeka, KS 66612
(913) 232-8265
(913) 233-4867 FAX
Specialty: C,G,M
Job Referral Service

JOB SEEKERS SURVIVAL HINTS

Area Code Problems?

The Bell System has recently added new area codes to certain metropolitan areas. Portions of the Los Angeles area including Santa Monica was assigned a new (310) area code and a number of other codes were changed in the suburban area. Northern California has a new (510) area code and Georgia a new (706) area code. While many of the firms listed in the SourceBook have supplied or verified the telephone number furnished, several of these area code changes were effective throughout 1992 making the verification process most difficult.

When you call a telephone number furnished by the SourceBook, it is possible that you will either be told you need to change the area code (in this instance the new area code is furnished) or that your call cannot be completed as dialed. The message received seems to relate to the recency of the implementation of the area code change. To clarify the area code check with your local Bell System operator.

PLAINS STATES JOB SEEKERS SOURCEBOOK

Section 7

Career Consultant Services

Overview

Career consultants generally offer assistance to job seekers for a fee. The range of their services extends from simple resume preparation, psychological counseling, vocational testing, interview practice videotaping, to coaching on every aspect of a job search.

Career consultants provide the most benefit in helping a job seeker to focus their efforts constructively to obtain a new job or make a career change in the shortest period of time.

The majority of these career services provide tools to help a job seeker, but still require each individual to actively direct their own job search.

Professionals in this field should have the appropriate educational background and sufficient experience to provide the services required. Generally, they are likely to have a Masters degree or higher accompanied with substantial practical experience.

In your selection process, look for firms that will take the time and care to pre-screen an individual at no charge to determine their needs.

Career consultants offer a variety of services at costs that range from relatively inexpensive to expensive. You can expect to pay from $50 to $125 per hour on an hourly basis. Avoid paying for package deals that are not necessary.

Look for consultants that have your best interests as their priority, instead of the fees to be earned. Good consultants will not attempt to sell services not needed or requested by an individual.

To assist you in your endeavors to find a qualified career consultant or counselor, we have provided important information on the following pages for the selection and use of these types of services.

How to Select a Career Consultant

Finding the right career consultant for you can take time and careful research. This process should not be rushed, since in most cases it is the individual that pays for their services. As with anything, the benefits derived are proportional to amount of effort applied.

This selection process cannot and should not be ignored. To maximize your chances of obtaining a job by using a career counselor/consultant means that you must work hard to qualify and then select a the right one.

Your goal is to find one that will provide the most beneficial services to support you during your job search. To assist you in this process we've outlined some important selection criteria below that should be useful.

Selection Criteria:

The selection of the right career counselor/consultant to support your job search efforts should be based upon a combination of the following criteria:

Proximity Is the firm convenient for you to visit on a regular basis?

This is important when attempting to meet on a regular basis to work through the issues on your job search.

Specialty   Does the consultant specialize in working with personnel in your career field and industry?

If so, they will be best able to understand your needs and will be the most experienced in providing you with useful information on how to find a new job. If they deal exclusively in your discipline, so much the better.

Experience   How long has the career counselor/consultant been in the business? And how long have they been working with members of your profession?

It is best to select a consultant who has at least three years experience specializing in your industry. These people will already have established a network of contacts with a number of hiring companies and will be better sources of information about new job

Personality   Does the consultant like you and do you like them? Do you "click" with the consultant?

If, yes, then you have a better shot at establishing and maintaining a good rapport with them on an ongoing basis.

Referrals   Was this firm referred to you by someone else in your field?

In addition to positive responses for the preceding qualifiers, a referral will give you a better feeling about their professional ability.

Quality Does this firm have a good reputation and do the consultants present themselves in a professional manner?

The best way to determine this is to talk to other job seekers and to visit the consultant's office to get a feeling for how the service is performed. If you're unhappy with what you see or find, keep looking.

Credentials Does this consultant have the proper education and work experience to be of meaningful assistance to you?

If not, then keep looking. Remember, this is a service that you are paying for, so don't settle on less than the best.

Questions to ask to qualify a career consultant:

1. How long have they been in the business?

    The longer a firm has been in the business, the more contacts they are likely to have, therefore increasing the odds that the service will truly facilitate your job search.

2. How many job seekers are they working with?

    Avoid career consultants that have more than 20 active job seekers per counselor, because you'll be easily forgotten.

3. Do they belong to any national or local professional affiliations?

    Qualified career consultants will usually belong to at least one professional organization. In many cases, membership in these organizations requires that a member meet certain educational or experience requirements.

5. What is the cost of their service? What are the hidden costs?

    Look for those services which charge on an hourly basis, with additional charges for other services as needed. With these firms you have better control over your long term costs by only paying for what you need as opposed to one price for a "package".

 Working with a Career Consultant

To maximize your success of having a career counselor/consultant to help you direct your professional career or find a new job, you need to remember a few important axioms.

 Career counselor/consultants normally charge a package fee or an hourly rate for services.

Therefore, do everything possible to help make their job easier. This includes having a very good resume available for their use and being prepared and on time for your work sessions with them.

 Good career consultants know their job, but they don't know you or how well you can perform your job.

This means that they need your help in getting to know you. Remember, you know your work history, skills, qualifications, and accomplishments best, so tell them what you are good at.

Describe and identify the important features of previous accomplishments. Furnish them with a means of measuring performance, such as a list of recognition awards or reference letters.

Career counselors/consultants are support personnel who will help you make decisions and focus your efforts to change careers or find a job.

The leg work to find a job is still your responsibility.

Career councelors/consultants really don't find people jobs, however their professional advice can be helpful in assisting you to find a job quicker.

If a consultant firm doesn't have the experience in your field or doesn't assist people in your particular circumstances, it may not be the firm for you to use.

If they have too many job seekers that they are attempting to serve, then they may be not be the best firm for you to use.

To find the best career consultant or counselor, do some comparison shopping and check references. Reputable firms will have many very good references and will gladly provide them to you.

Review any contract carefully before signing. It should be clear as to what services you will be provided, for the fee that you are paying.

Finally, the ultimate responsibility for handling a career change or finding a job is still your obligation. It requires that you work hard at this task. Using a career consultant is not a passive activity.

Office Manager
A A D & K Fortis
2900 E 26th Street Ste 313
Sioux Falls, SD 57103
(605) 339-0052
Specialty: G
Career & Vocational Counseling

Office Manager
Aaron-Leary Leigh
8020 E Central
Wichita, KS 67206
(316) 634-0029
Specialty: G
Career & Vocational Counseling

Office Manager
Accomplished Resume Services
2921 SW Wanamker Drive
Topeka, KS 66614
(913) 273-5112
Specialty: G
Career & Vocational Counseling

Office Manager
Advanced Career Network
8000 W 110th St Ste 150
Shawnee Mission, KS 66210
(913) 339-6999
Specialty: G
Career & Vocational Counseling

Office Manager
Andrew Schauer PhD
5847 SW 29
Topeka, KS 66614
(913) 273-7292
Specialty: G
Career & Vocational Counseling

Office Manager
Associated Personnel Techs
1219 E Douglas Ave
Wichita, KS 67211
(316) 264-0681
Specialty: G
Career & Vocational Counseling

Office Manager
Associates For Personal Growth
8980 Hickman Ste 210
Des Monies, IA 50325
(515) 252-0440
Specialty: Interest/Skills
Indentification
Career & Vocational Counseling

Office Manager
Availability Employment
1521 S Minnesota Ave
Sioux Falls, SD 57105
(605) 336-0353
Specialty: G
Career & Vocational Counseling

Office Manager
Bernard Haldane Associates
121 Whittier Street
Wichita, KS 67207
(316) 689-6868
Specialty: Job Search Guidance
Career & Vocational Counseling

Office Manager
Bier Marilyn
8575 W 110th St
Shawnee Mission, KS 66210
(913) 451-1900
Specialty: G
Career & Vocational Counseling

Office Manager
Business & Banking Institute
609 Merle Hay Tower
Des Moines, IA 50310
(515) 270-2750
Specialty: B
Career & Vocational Counseling

Office Manager
Business & Banking Institute
7101 Mercy Road
Omaha, NE 68106
(401) 393-1428
Specialty: B
Career & Vocational Counseling

Office Manager
C D I Career Development
2605 W 37th Street
Sioux Falls, SD 57105
(605) 334-9779
Specialty: G
Career & Vocational Counseling

Office Manager
Career Centers Inc
7602 Pacific Street LL 103
Omaha, NB 68114
(401) 399-2070
Specialty: Career Fairs-Employer Contacts
Career Counseling/
Corporate Outplacement

Office Manager
Career Design Inc
12020 Shamrock Plaza
Omaha, NB 68154
(401) 333-8484
Specialty: Career Planning
Career & Vocational Counseling

Office Manager
Career Directions Ltd
2701 SE Convenience Blvd Ste 3
Ankeny, IA 50021
(515) 964-2654
Specialty: Life Planning Services
Career & Vocational Counseling

Patrick A O'Malley PdD, Pres
Career Dynamics Inc
11111 W 95th St
Overland Park, KS 66214

(913) 492-9191
(913) 492-9197 FAX

Specialty: G

- OutplacementCounseling
- Job Search Services
- Employment Testing
- Career & Jobs Development

Career/Outplacement Consulting

Office Manager
Career Learning Center
310 11th Street W
Lemmon, SD 57638
(605) 374-5858
Specialty: G
Career & Vocational Counseling

Donna Gregory, Career Advisor
Career Learning Center
110 2nd Street West
Mobridge, SD 57601
(605) 845-7377
Specialty: Pre-Employment Training
Career & Vocational Counseling

Vaughn L Carter, Pres
Career Management Services
5000 Central Park Drive Ste 204
Lincoln, NE 68504

(402) 466-8427
(402) 466-5933 FAX

Specialty: Job Search Counseling

- Complete Job Search Counseling
- Resume Development And Use
- Position Identification
- Power Interviewing
- Career Management

Career Consultant Service

Office Manager
Career Planners
9948 W 87th St
Overland Park, KS 66212
(913) 649-1112
Specialty: G
Career & Vocational Counseling

Office Manager
Career Planning Center
421 S Main Street
Aberdeen, SD 57401
(605) 622-2298
Specialty: G
Career & Vocational Counseling

Office Manager
Career Quest
P O Box 10404
Bettendorf, IA 52722
(319) 388-9380
Specialty: G
Career & Vocational Counseling

Office Manager
Career Transition Specialists
10550 Barkley St
Shawnee Mission, KS 66212
(913) 383-9192
Specialty: G
Career & Vocational Counseling

Office Manager
Carr & Assoc
10880 Benson St Ste 2330
Shawnee Mission, KS 66210
(913) 451-9220
Specialty: G
Career & Vocational Counseling

Office Manager
Cedar River Psychological Services
417 1 Avenue SE
Cedar Rapids, IA 52401
(401) 366-6329
Specialty: G
Career & Vocational Counseling

Office Manager
Changes
229 E William St
Wichita, KS 67202
(316) 263-1166
Specialty: G
Career & Vocational Counseling

Office Manager
Creative Careers
1001 Av NE-Lower Level
Cedar Rapids IA 52401
(319) 366-1338
Specialty: Mid Life Career
Change, Career Workshops
Career & Vocational Counseling

Office Manager
Don Thomas Blasi
641 S Hillside Street
Wichita, KS 67211
(316) 684-2422
Specialty: Work Life Task
Interview
Career & Vocational Counseling

Office Manager
Employment Consultants Inc
204 Collins Road NE Ste 203
Cedar Rapids, IA 52402
(401) 377-7344
Specialty: Confidence Building
Career & Vocational Counseling

Jerald Marshall, VP Rehabilation
**Goodwill Industries
Rehabilitation Facility**
P O Box 1438
Sioux City, IA 51102
(712) 258-4511
(712) 258-7832
Specialty: Job Search Assistance,
Vocational Rehabilitation
Career Consultant

Office Manager
Gus Shoffner
205 Galvin Road N
Bellevue, NE 68005
(401) 291-7712
Specialty: G
Career & Vocational Counseling

Judith Davies, Sr VP
**Human Resource Management
Corp**
2120 S 72nd St Suite 620
Omaha, NE 68124
(402) 399-8944
(402) 393-4286 FAX
Specialty: Organizational
& Career Assessment
Career Consulting

Office Manager
Iowa State University
10861 Douglas Ave
Urbandale, IA 50322
(515) 270-8114
Specialty: G
Career & Vocational Counseling

Office Manager
James M Brodie PhD
809 South Street
Rapid City, SD 57701
(605) 348-8000
Specialty: G
Career & Vocational Counseling

Office Manager
Job Training Program
315 5th Ave S
Clinton, IA 52732
(319) 243-9060
Specialty: G
Career & Vocational Counseling

Office Manager
John Joseph Group
7000 W Center Rd Suite 100
Omaha, NE 68144
(402) 399-9763
Specialty: Formalized Job
Lead Program
Human Resource Consulting/
Outplacement Programs

Office Manager
Johnson Ronald Phd
628 1st Ave
Council Bluffs, IA 51501
(712) 323-1288
Specialty: G
Career & Vocational Counseling

Office Manager
Kessler & Assoc
6818 Grover St Ste 304
Omaha, NE 68106
(402) 397-9558
Specialty: G
Career & Vocational Counseling

Joy Harvey, Outplacement Manager
Key Outplacement Services
1001 Office Park Road
West Des Moines, IA 50265-2567
(515) 224-0446
(515) 224-6599 FAX
Specialty: G
Career/Outplacement Counseling

Daniel M Kirkhuff, Employment Consultant
Kirkhuff Personnel System
949 South Glendale Ste 125
Wichita, KS 67218
(316) 685-5236
Specialty: G
Career Consultant Service

Office Manager
Labette Community College
200 S 14th St
Parsons, KS 67357
(316) 421-6700
Specialty: G
Career & Vocational Counseling

Office Manager
Life Works
2010 S Ankeny Blvd
Ankeny, IA 50021
(515) 964-6710
Specialty: Group Courses
Career & Vocational Counseling

Office Manager
Manhattan Area Vocational Tech
3136 Dickens Ave
Manhattan, KS 66502
(913) 539-7431
Specialty: G
Career & Vocational Counseling

Office Manager
Martin Kate & Associates
400 N Woodlawn Street
Wichita, KS 67208
(316) 652-7400
Specialty: Re-Careering
Career & Vocational Counseling

Office Manager
Midlands Psychological Assoc
15770 Q St
Omaha, NE 68135
(402) 896-5131
Specialty: G
Career & Vocational Counseling

Office Manager
Midwest Career Development Service
754 N 31st St
Kansas City, KS 66102
(913) 621-6348
Specialty: G
Career & Vocational Counseling

Office Manager
Mullin & Assoc
1916 Nash Dr
Des Moines, IA 50314
(515) 284-5250
Specialty: G
Career & Vocational Counseling

Office Manager
Nebraska Dept of Education
2727 W 2nd St Ste 470
Hastings, NE 68901
(402) 462-5193
Specialty: G
Career & Vocational Counseling

Office Manager
Noll-Selection Testing
900 Commercial Federal Tower
Omaha, NE 68124
(402) 391-7736
Specialty: G
Career & Vocational Counseling

Office Manager
Nordine & Associates
1701 22 Street Ste 201
West Des Moines, IA 50310
(515) 223-5511
Specialty: Career Assessment
Career & Vocational Counseling

Sharon Strong, Coordinator
Older Worker Employment
124 W 46th Street
Kearney, NE 68847
(308) 234-1851
(308) 234-1853 FAX
Specialty: Job Search Referral Consultant
South Central NE Area Agency On Aging

Office Manager
Professional Resource Ctr
10500 Barkley St
Shawnee Mission, KS 66212
(913) 381-4484
Specialty: G
Career & Vocational Counseling

Office Manager
Quality Rehabiltation Services Inc
11640 Arbor Ste 100
Omaha, NE 68130
(401) 333-2543
Specialty: G
Career & Vocational Counseling

Office Manager
Rehabilitation Professionals
10822 Old Mill Rd Ste 1
Omaha, NE 68154
(402) 333-3052
Specialty: G
Career & Vocational Counseling

Office Manager
Reynolds & Associates
1200 35 Street
West Des Moines, IA 50260
(515) 223-1892
Specialty: G
Career & Vocational Counseling

Office Manager
Sioux Falls College
1501 S Prairie Ave
Sioux Falls, SD 57105
(605) 331-6697
Specialty: G
Career & Vocational Counseling

Office Manager
Siouxland Evaluation Services
2600 Military Road
Sioux City, IA 51103
(712) 258-1781
Specialty: G
Career & Vocational Counseling

Twila F Deahl, Owner
The Career Connection
1621 S University Drive Ste 215
Fargo, ND 58103
(701) 232-4614
(701) 241-9822 FAX
Specialty: C,E,F,M
Career Consultant Service

Office Manager
TRS
8902 W 104th Terr
Shawnee Mission, KS 66212
(913) 341-5348
Specialty: G
Career & Vocational Counseling

Gayle M Tichauer
Vocational Assessment Services Inc
10730 Pacific Street Ste 33
Omaha, NE 68114
(401) 390-9950
Specialty: G
Career & Vocational Counseling

Office Manager
Vocational Economics Inc
250 N Kansas
Wichita, KS 67214
(316) 291-3604
Specialty: Career Counseling & Life Planning
Career & Vocational Counseling

Office Manager
Wichita Growth Ctr
641 S Hillside St
Wichita, KS 67211
(316) 684-2422
Specialty: G
Career & Vocational Counseling

Office Manager
William Hercher
110 N Market
Wichita, KS 67202
(316) 262-8268
Specialty: G
Career & Vocational Counseling

PLAINS STATES
JOB SEEKERS SOURCEBOOK

Section 8

Outplacement Services

Overview

Outplacement services generally offer assistance to job seekers for a fee that is usually paid for by one's previous employer (Corporate Sponsored).

The range of their services extends from simple resume preparation, vocational testing, use of an office (complete with telephone and secretarial support), to coaching on every aspect of the job search.

Outplacement services offer a variety of services at costs that range from relatively inexpensive to expensive. In the majority of the cases, the cost of such services is covered by the previous employer, especially if the employer has just gone through a restructuring.

The value of any of these services to a job seeker depends upon several things: the quality of the service, the kind of work being sought, the access or exposure that these services have to hiring companies and your own level of experience.

It should be noted that outplacement services provide the most benefit by helping job seekers focus their efforts constructively to obtain new jobs in the shortest period of time.

Outplacement services provide the tools to help job seekers expedite their job search, but still require individuals to actively direct their own job search.

The next few pages contain important information on how to:

- Select an outplacement service for help

- Work with an outplacement service for maximum results

How to Select an Outplacement Service

Finding the right outplacement firm for you can take time and careful research. This process should not be rushed, since different firms offer distinct levels of outplacement support at a variety of different costs.

Taking time to pick the right service will ensure that you are satisfied that you are getting the best service for the money spent, regardless as to who is paying the fee.

This careful selection process cannot and should not be ignored. To maximize your chances of obtaining a job with the aid of an outplacement firm means that you must work hard to qualify and then select a service that provides the most beneficial service package to support your job search efforts.

To assist you in this process we've outlined some important selection criteria below.

Selection Criteria:

The selection of the best outplacement firm to support your job search efforts should be based upon a combination of the following criteria:

Specialty Does the consultant specialize in working with personnel in your career field and industry?

If so, they will most likely be better prepared to understand your needs and will be the most helpful in providing you with useful information on how and where to find a new job. If they deal exclusively in your discipline, so much the better.

Experience How long has this outplacement firm been in the business? And how long have they been working with members of your profession?

It is best to select an outplacement firm that has at least three years experience specializing in your industry. Seasoned firms will have an established network of contacts with a number of hiring companies and should be a better source for assisting you to locate job openings.

Personality Does the outplacement consultant like you and do you like them? Do you "click"?

If yes, then you have a better shot at establishing and maintaining a good rapport with them on an ongoing basis. This is especially important for those times when you have a need to discuss potential job offers or personal family matters related to your career change or job search.

Proximity Is the firm convenient for you to visit on a regular basis?

This is important since many of the services provided by an outplacement firm are only provided on premise.

Quality	Does this firm have a good reputation and do they present themselves in a professional manner?
	The best way to determine this is to talk to other job seekers and to visit the outplacement firm's office to size them up. If you're unhappy with what you see or find, keep looking. If your employer is paying the fee then have a discussion with your Human Resources department about your observations and conclusions.
Cost	How much does this service cost?
	Evaluate the services received against your cost.
Referrals	Was this firm referred to you by someone else?
	Given that you have positive responses for the preceding qualifiers, a referral will give you a better feeling about their professional ability.
Background	Does this consultant have the proper education and work experience to be of meaningful assistance to you?
	If not, then keep looking. Remember, this is a service that someone, maybe you, is paying for, so don't settle on less than the best.

Questions to ask to qualify an outplacement service:

1. How long have they been in the business?

   The longer a firm has been in the business, the more contacts they are likely to have, therefore the odds of their being able to help you are better.

2. Number of job seekers in your field that they work with monthly?

   Firms handling a minimum of five people in your field per month are best suited to help you manage your career change.

3. How many job seekers are they working with?

   Avoid those firms that have more than 30 active job seekers per counselor, because you'll be easily forgotten.

4. How many client companies are they working with?

   Firms which average two or three companies per counselor are about the right size to support you in your job search. Those firms attempting to handle a larger number of hiring companies per counselor may be spreading their resources too thin.

5. What services do they provide and for how long?

Outplacement firms differ widely in the type, quality, and amount of services which they provide to their clients.

Many of them just offer their services to corporate sponsors.

It is very important to find the firm that provides the best range of services for the least cost.

Working with an Outplacement Firm

To maximize your success of having an outplacement firm help you redirect your professional career or find a new job, you need to remember a few important axioms.

Outplacement firms normally get paid a package fee or a hourly rate for their services.

Therefore, do everything possible to make it easier for them to help you. This includes having a very good resume available for their use, being prepared and on time for your work sessions with them.

Good outplacement firms know their job, but they don't know you or how well you can perform on the job.

To do their job right, they will need your help in getting to know you. Be cooperative in completing assignments, furnishing information, and applying techniques learned.

In addition to supplying the typical day to day support, these services often offer training in various job search methodologies -- <u>apply what you learn</u>.

Outplacement Services

Recap:

If an outplacement firm doesn't have the experience in your field, it may not be the firm for you to use.

If the firm have too many job seekers that they are attempting to serve, then they may be not be the best firm for you to use.

Using a good qualified outplacement firm can be very beneficial to help initiate, organize, and execute a job search.

To find the best firm for your needs, do some comparison shopping and check references. Any reputable firm will gladly provide them for you.

An outplacement firm is a service designed to facilitate your job search efforts, but putting the effort into finding a job is still the <u>job seeker's responsibility</u>.

Office Manager
American Management Resources
3408 Woodland Avenue Ste 401
West Des Moines, IA 50266
(515) 222-9044
Specialty: G
Outplacement Consultant

Office Manager
Cambridge Permanent Employment
Cedar River Tower
First Avenue & First Street NE
Cedar Rapids, IA 52401-1134
(712) 366-7771
Specialty: B,C,F,E,H,O,S
Outplacement Consultant

Office Manager
Career Centers Inc
7602 Pacific Street LL 103
Omaha, NB 68114
(401) 399-2070
Specialty: Career Fairs-Employer Contacts
Career Counseling/
Corporate Outplacement

Patrick A O'Malley PdD, Pres
Career Dynamics Inc
11111 W 95th St
Overland Park, KS 66214

(913) 492-9191
(913) 492-9197 FAX

Specialty: G

- OutplacementCounseling
- Job Search Services
- Employment Testing
- Career & Jobs Development

Career/Outplacement Consulting

Vaughn L Carter, Pres
Career Management Services
5000 Central Park Drive Ste 204
Lincoln, NE 68504

(402) 466-8427
(402) 466-5933 FAX

Specialty: Job Search Counseling/ Career Management
- Complete Job Search Counseling
- Resume Development And Use
- Position Identification
- Power Interviewing

Outplacment, Individual or Corporate

Office Manager
Challenger Gray & Christmas
10540 Marty St
Shawnee Mission, KS 66212
(913) 341-7043
Specialty: G
Outplacement Firm

Office Manager
Deems Associates
2701 SE Convenience Blvd Ste 3
Ankeny, IA 50021
(515) 964-0219
Specialty: G
Outplacement Consultant

Office Manager
Hercher WM E
110 N Market St
Wichita, KS 67202
(316) 262-8268
Specialty: G
Outplacement Consultants

Judith Davies, Sr VP
Human Resource Management Corp
2120 S 72nd St Suite 620
Omaha, NE 68124
(402) 399-8944
(402) 393-4286 FAX
Specialty: Organizational
& Career Assessment
Corporate Sponsored
Outplacement

Joy Harvey, Manager
Key Outplacement Services
1001 Office Park Road
West Des Moines, IA 50265-2567
(515) 224-0446
(515) 224-6599 FAX
Specialty: G
Career/Outplacement Counseling

Office Manager
Managment Resource Group
400 Main Street
Davenport, IA 52801
(515) 424-1680
Specialty: G
Outplacement Counseling

Office Manager
P S Agency
250 N Rock Rd
Wichita, KS 67206
(316) 686-6529
Specialty: G
Outplacement Consultants

Office Manager
Right Assoc
3500 N Rock Rd
Wichita, KS 67226
(316) 636-2038
Specialty: G
Outplacement Firm

Jack L Shafer, VP
The John Joseph Group Ltd
7000 W Center Rd Suite 100
Omaha, NE 68106

(402) 399-9763
(402) 399-9031 FAX

Specialty: Outplacement Counseling

- Group and Executive Programs
- Manager Notifier Training
- Private Offices & Workstations
- Offices In Major Cities
- Full Range of Administrative Services

Human Resource Consulting/ Outplacement Programs

Office Manager
The Park Group
2556 NE 96 Avenue
Ankeny, IA 50021
(515) 965-0366
Specialty: G
Outplacement Consultant

PLAINS STATES
JOB SEEKERS SOURCEBOOK

Section 9

Resume Preparation Services

Resume preparation firms help an individual prepare a professional looking resume for making the best impression on hiring companies. As such, these firms vary in the services that they offer.

Some provide just simple typing and copying support. Others offer resume preparation using a laser printer that offers a variety of type fonts to create a better appearance.

Still others have developed a carefully thought out approach to the preparation of a structured resume. These types of services use professional writers to enhance the presentation of an individual's job history. These firms also charge more, but they put much more effort into the creation and printing of a document that will gain attention to help you obtain a job sooner.

Spending a little time to comparison shop and review samples of their work will pay off in the long haul. Your resume is your first, and sometimes the only, opportunity to make an impression. The right firm will get the job done for you, but your input is critical to the successful creation of this product.

The next few pages contain important information which will assist you in understanding how to:

- Select a resume preparation firm to help you

- Work with a resume preparation firm

How to Select a Resume Preparation Service

Finding the correct resume preparation service is a fairly easy task, given that you spend a little time on advance research. This process should not be bypassed, since having a professional looking resume is the most important first step of any job search.

To maximize your chances of selecting the best resume preparation service to meet your needs, you must first determine what are your needs and then qualify a service according to THESE needs. To assist you in this process we've outlined some useful selection criteria.

Selection Criteria:

The selection of the right resume preparation service to use to prepare a professional looking resume should be based upon a combination of the following criteria:

Experience   How long has the resume preparation service been in the business?

It is best to select a service that has at least three years experience specializing in preparing resumes. These people will already have established a good reputation and will most likely know how to assist you in creating that best first impression on paper.

Proximity Is the service convenient for you to visit several times?

This is important when attempting to meet to proof your resume and when it is necessary to obtain additional copies of your resume.

Personality Do you "click" with the resume preparer?

If, yes, then you have a better shot at establishing and maintaining a good rapport with them and in obtaining the best prepared resume.

Referrals Was this firm referred to you by someone else?

Given that you have positive responses for the preceding qualifiers, a referral will give you a better feeling about their professional ability.

Quality Does this agency have a good reputation and do they present themselves in a professional manner?

The best way to determine this is to talk to other job seekers and to visit the resume preparer's office to size them up. If you're unhappy with what you see or find, keep looking.

Services What services are provided by the resume preparer?

Some firms just do typing and formatting, others provide full service support which includes a detailed evaluation of your work history. The latter of these firms tend to provide a better service for those people inexperienced in putting together a good resume.

Networks Is this consultant a member of a professional affiliation?

If yes, then the chances are that they must meet some level of professional standards for their industry. This in turn usually means that they are experienced and qualified enough to be able to do a good job on your resume.

Cost What is the total cost of the service?

It is important to understand what your cost is in relationship to the services being provided. Full service firms that spend time to analyze your job history and work with you one-on-one should cost more that just a typing service.

Questions you should ask to qualify a resume preparation firm:

1. How long have they been in the business?

    The longer a firm has been in the business, the more experience that they are likely to have, therefore the odds of their being able to help you are better.

2. How many job seekers from your field have they worked with?

    Firms handling a large number of people in your field will best understand some of the buzz words in the industry and be less prone to make mistakes when preparing your resume.

3. How much does this service cost? And how long will it take?

    Look for the hidden costs such as costs for extra copies of resumes. Find out if there is a charge for rush orders or delivery.

4. Are they able to offer you a variety of type fonts and sizes to customize your resume?

    The better services will have this capability.

5. What is the background of the staff you will be working with?

    Finding a service which has experience in career consulting and professional writing would be the best choice to serve your needs if you need more than just typing.

Working with a Resume Preparation Firm

To succeed in having a resume preparation firm do a good job for you when preparing your resume, you need to remember a few important points.

Resume preparation firms normally get paid a package fee for their services.

Therefore, do everything possible to help make their job easier. This includes having a good write up of your job history available for their use, being prepared and on time for your work sessions with them.

Good resume preparation firms know their job, but they don't know anything about you or your work background.

To provide you with the best possible service they need your help in documenting your work history. Remember, you know your work experience better than anyone, so tell them what you are good at.

Identify and describe in detail the important features of previous accomplishments. Furnish specific information for measuring performance, such as a list of recognition awards or reference letters.

The final product is your responsibility.

Therefore, proof and reproof each version of the resume until you are completely satisfied. Check font types, margin spacing, and the alignment of similar entries.

K.I.S.S. (Keep it simple stupid)

Avoid having your resume appear too cluttered, be specific, and if needed allow your resume to go to two pages (but never three).

If a resume preparation firm hasn't been in business very long, it may not be the firm for you to use.

Finally, review any contract carefully before signing. It should be clear as to what services you will be provided for the fee that you are paying.

P Michael Young
" A " Executive Writing Services
7701 Pacific Suite 111
Omaha, NE 68108
(402) 399-9853
Specialty: Desktop Publishing, Composition, Editing
Resume Preparation Service

Office Manager
A-1 Resume Services
1138 37 Street
Des Moines, IA 50311
(515) 277-2219
Specialty: Write,Edit,Layout
Resume Service

Office Manager
A Appletree Resume & Writing Professionals
1917 S Minnesota Avenue
Sioux Falls, SD 57105
(605) 336-2322
Specialty: Writing-Layout-Printing
Resume Service

Office Manager
AAA Resume Service
2545 Williams Avenue
Sioux City, IA 51106
(712) 276-6517
Specialty: Professionally Written & Printed
Resume Service

Office Manager
A Better Resume Service
2127 5th Avenue
Moline, IL 61265
(309) 764-2470
Specialty: Free Consultation
Resume Service

Office Manager
Accell Resume
7008 W 83rd St
Shawnee Mission, KS 66204
(913) 649-8973
Specialty: G
Resume Service

Office Manager
A Plus Resume & Writing Services
3009 Merle Hay Road
Des Moines, IA 50310
(515) 253-0926
Specialty: Writing,Formatting & Printing
Resume Service

Office Manager
Accomplished Resume Services
2921 SW Wanamaker Drive
Topeka, KS 66614
(913) 273-5112
Specialty: Redesign & Update Service
Resume Service

Office Manager
Action Career Tactics
5000 Johnson Dr
Shawnee Mission, KS 66205
(913) 432-1096
Specialty: G
Resume Service

Office Manager
Advanced Business Services
2214 Aspen Dr
Dubuque, IA 52001
(319) 582-0459
Specialty: G
Resume Service

Office Manager
Advanced Printing & Copy
533 N Lindenwood Dr
Olathe, KS 66062
(913) 764-5775
Specialty: G
Resume Service

Office Manager
Advanced Resume
5326 E Oakwood Dr
Pleasant Hill, IA 50317
(515) 265-2863
Specialty: G
Resume Service

Office Manager
Advantage Professional Svcs
707 N Waco
Wichita, KS 67203
(316) 263-3994
Specialty: G
Resume Service

Office Manager
Advantage Resumes
1820 S Lark
Wichita, KS 67209
(316) 722-6469
Specialty: G
Resume Service

Office Manager
Allegro Writing Svc
11800 Shawnee Mission Pky
Shawnee Mission, KS 66203
(913) 631-1505
Specialty: G
Resume Service

Office Manager
American Executive Svc
808 3rd Ave S Ste 1
Fargo, ND 58103
(701) 235-7918
Specialty: G
Resume Service

Office Manager
American Management Resources
3408 Woodland Ave Ste 401
West Des Moines, IA 50265
(515) 222-9044
Specialty: G
Resume Service

Office Manager
Appletree's Resume & Writing
3309 Fiechtner Dr SW Ste F
Fargo, ND 58103
(701) 232-1262
Specialty: G
Resume Service

Office Manager
Associated Personnel Svc
1220 E Capital Ave
Grand Island, NE 68801
(308) 384-4885
Specialty: G
Resume Service

Office Manager
At Your Service Assoc
8600 W 95th St
Shawnee Mission, KS 66212
(913) 341-7766
Specialty: G
Resume Service

Office Manager
Audrey's Typing & Word Processing
9140 W Dodge Rd
Omaha, NE 68114
(402) 397-0617
Specialty: G
Resume Service

Office Manager
Backman Resume Svc
9037 W 101st Ter
Shawnee Mission, KS 66212
(913) 341-1020
Specialty: G
Resume Service

Office Manager
Bellevue Copy Center
806 Fort Crook Rd
Bellevue, NE 68005
(402) 291-7744
Specialty: G
Resume Service

Office Manager
Bellevue Personnel Resume Services
1820 Hillcrest Dr
Bellevue, NE 68005
(402) 291-6611
Specialty: G
Resume Service

Office Manager
Bismarck Reminder Inc
106 E Thayer Ave
Bismarck, ND 58501
(701) 223-2180
Specialty: G
Resume Service

Claudia Stephenson, Manager
Bismarck Secretarial Service
206 E Broadway Ave
Bismarck, ND 58501
(701) 255-3141
(701) 258-7888 FAX
Specialty: Resumes, Letters, Applications
Resume Preparation Service

Office Manager
Brent & Assoc
12205 Shawnee Mission Pky
Shawnee Mission, KS 66216
(913) 962-0285
Specialty: G
Resume Service

Office Manager
Caraway Printing
204 N Main St
Lansing, KS 66043
(913) 727-5223
Specialty: G
Resume Service

Vaughn L Carter, Pres
Career Management Services
5000 Central Park Drive Ste 204
Lincoln, NE 68504

(402) 466-8427
(402) 466-5933 FAX

Specialty: Job Search Counseling

- Complete Job Search Counseling
- Resume Development And Use
- Position Identification
- Power Interviewing
- Career Management

Resume Prepartion Service

Office Manager
Career Network
1131 Westrac Dr Ste 202
Fargo, ND 58103
(701) 237-6931
Specialty: G
Resume Service

Office Manager
Career Network
1407 24th Ave S Ste 217
Grand Forks, ND 58201
(701) 775-2808
Specialty: G
Resume Service

Office Manager
Career Resources
820 1 Street
West Des Moines, IA 50265
(515) 255-4923
Specialty: G
Resume Service

Nita Ridley, Editor/Writer
Career Trend Resumes
6800 College Blvd Ste 555
Overland Park, KS 66211
(913) 451-1313
(913) 491-3434 FAX
Specialty: Laser Printing,
Consulting(Free)
Resume Writing Service

Office Manager
CareerPro Resume
42 & Center Mall Suite 123
Omaha, NE 68105
(402) 345-2425
Specialty: G
Resume Service

Office Manager
CareerPro Resumes
Duck Creek Plaza Bank Building
Suite 270
Bettendorf, IA 52722
(319) 359-6515
Specialty: Complete Marketing
Packages
Resume Service

Office Manager
Clerical/Secretarial Svc
410 S Lyndale Ave
Sioux Falls, SD 57104
(605) 338-4206
Specialty: G
Resume Service

Office Manager
Colonial Park Business Svc
1901 Broadway Ave
Iowa City, IA 52240
(319) 338-8800
Specialty: G
Resume Service

Office Manager
Compuprint
5407 W 41st Street
Sioux Falls, SD 57106
(605) 361-6720
Specialty: G
Resume Service

Office Manager
Computer Resource Center
803 N Main
Minoit, ND 58701
(605) 852-1080
Specialty: G
Resume Service

Office Manager
Cooper Videographics
2026 E 29th St
Scottsbluff, NE 69361
(308) 632-4758
Specialty: G
Resume Service

Office Manager
Copy Works
105 Welch Street
Ames, IA 50010
(515) 292-3630
Specialty: Resumes & Cover Letters
Resume Service

Office Manager
Costello & Assoc
4210 S 33rd St Ste G
Lincoln, NE 68506
(402) 483-7611
Specialty: G
Resume Service

Office Manager
Courtesy Business Service
702 W 11 Street
Sioux Falls, SD 57104
(605) 338-3441
Specialty: G
Resume Service

Office Manager
Creative Computer Svc
112 N Wheeler Ave
Grand Island, NE 68801
(308) 381-1627
Specialty: G
Resume Service

Office Manager
Darlene's
216 N Bailey Ave
North Platte, NE 69101
(308) 534-8717
Specialty: G
Resume Service

Office Manager
Data Designers
3000 2nd Av
Kearny, NE 68847
(308) 234-5966
Specialty: G
Resume Service

Office Manager
Dick Hoff Typing
1010 8th Ave N
Clinton, IA 52732
(319) 242-7359
Specialty: G
Resume Service

Office Manager
Dickinson Secretarial Svc
513 Elks Dr
Dickinson, ND 58601
(701) 225-9172
Specialty: G
Resume Service

Office Manager
DME Secretarial Services
3549 Southern Hills Drive
Sioux City, IA 51106
(712) 274-8642
Specialty: G
Resume Service

Office Manager
Edsall's Printing Svc
1202 S 3rd Ave
Marshalltown, IA 50158
(515) 753-8920
Specialty: G
Resume Service

Office Manager
Empire Word Processing
4320 Louise Ave Ste 102
Sioux Falls, SD 57106
(605) 361-4151
Specialty: G
Resume Service

Office Manager
Employment Consultants
204 Collins Rd NE Suite 203
Cedar Rapids, IA 52402
(319) 377-7344
Specialty: G
Resume Service

Office Manager
Executive Secretarial Svc
2630 Jackson Blvd Ste 103
Rapid City, SD 57702
(605) 343-2921
Specialty: G
Resume Service

Office Manager
Executive Secretarial Svcs
3593 5th Ave S
Fort Dodge, IA 50501
(515) 955-8333
Specialty: G
Resume Service

Office Manager
Express Copy Shop
2317 W 12 Street
Sioux Falls, SD 57104
(605) 332-2484
Specialty: G
Resume Service

Office Manager
Expressway Personnel
523 E Bismarck Expy
Bismarck, ND 58504
(701) 222-0071
Specialty: G
Resume Service

Office Manager
First Impression Resumes
120 S Market
Wichita, KS 67202
(316) 264-8803
Specialty: G
Resume Service

Pete Flaming, Pres
**Flaming & Associates
Resume Division**
120 W 6th Street Ste 120
Newton, KS 67114
(316) 283-3851
(316) 283-3859 FAX
Specialty: G
Resume Preparation Service

Office Manager
General Office Svcs
613 Main St Ste 201
Rapid City, SD 57701
(605) 341-4728
Specialty: G
Resume Service

Office Manager
Graphics Plus
343 Colorado St
Manhattan, KS 66502
(913) 539-6027
Specialty: G
Resume Service

Office Manager
Ingle's Computer Service
105 Birch Ct
North Liberty, IA 52317
(319) 626-2528
Specialty: G
Resume Service

Office Manager
Integrated Services Ltd
417 1st Ave E
Williston, ND 58801
(701) 774-8484
Specialty: G
Resume Service

Office Manager
Ireland Design & Publishing
2016 College Street
Cedar Falls, IA 50613
(319) 277-8067
Specialty: 24 Hour Turnaround
Resume Service

Office Manager
Jean Barban Graphics
1260 27th Ave
Columbus, NE 68601
(402) 563-2690
Specialty: G
Resume Service

Office Manager
**Johnnie's Typing &
Secretarial**
110 E Madison St
Iola, KS 66749
(316) 365-2660
Specialty: G
Resume Service

Office Manager
Kingston Printing & Design
804 W 24th St
Lawrence, KS 66046
(913) 841-6320
Specialty: G
Resume Service

David Boardman, Desktop
Publishing Coordinator
Kinko's Copies
3109 W 41st Street Ste 217
Sioux Falls, SD 57105
(605) 333-0750
Specialty: Full & Self Service
Resume Service

Office Manager
KTS Publishing
502 E 13th St
Baxter Springs, KS 66713
(316) 856-3302
Specialty: G
Resume Service

Office Manager
L R Secretarial Svc
601 14th St
Hawarden, IA 51023
(712) 552-1450
Specialty: G
Resume Service

Office Manager
Layout & Design Concepts
1809 S Broadway
Minot, ND 58701
(605) 839-1224
Specialty: G
Resume Service

Office Manager
Letter Perfect
516 N Cedar St
Gardner, KS 66030
(913) 884-6200
Specialty: G
Resume Service

Naglii C Sassine, Pres
Lind's Printing Service Inc
332 S Clinton Street
Iowa City, IA 52240
(319) 337-7241
(319) 337-4422 FAX
Specialty: Resume Preparation & Laser Printing
Quality Printing Company

Office Manager
Mailboxes & Parcel Depot
102 E Kimberly Rd
Davenport, IA 52806
(319) 386-2900
Specialty: G
Resume Service

Office Manager
Mangement Recruiters
150 1st Av NE
Cedar Rapids, IA 52401
(319) 366-8441
Specialty: G
Resume Service

Office Manager
Maverick House Press
626 40th St
Rock Island, IL 61201
(309) 793-5006
Specialty: G
Resume Service

Office Manager
McKirchy & Company
PO Box 825
Bettendorf, IA 52722
(319) 332-8888
Specialty: G
Resume Service

Office Manager
MPC Computers & Graphics
26 S Main Street
Council Bluffs, IA 51503
(712) 325-8717
Specialty: G
Resume Service

Office Manager
Next Step
518 Nebraska St
Sioux City, IA 51101
(712) 255-9454
Specialty: G
Resume Service

Office Manager
Northwestern Printers
815 N Main St
Russell, KS 67665
(913) 483-6235
Specialty: G
Resume Service

Office Manager
Oakstone Consulting
1315 Jersey Ridge Rd Suite 1
Davenport, IA 52803
(319) 322-0515
Specialty: Laser Imprinted
Resume Service

Office Manager
Office Alternative
3033 13th Ave SW
Fargo, ND 58103
(701) 237-0277
Specialty: G
Resume Service

Sharon Strong, Coordinator
Older Worker Employment
124 W 46th Street
Kearney, NE 68847
(308) 234-1851
(308) 234-1853 FAX
Specialty: Job Search Referral
Consultant
South Central NE Area Agency
On Aging

Office Manager
P S Agency
250 N Rock Rd
Wichita, KS 67206
(316) 686-3975
Specialty: G
Resume Service

Office Manager
Parsec Enterprises
315 E 7th St
Hastings, NE 68901
(402) 463-7524
Specialty: G
Resume Service

Office Manager
Pechman Resume Service
508 S Clinton St
Iowa City, IA 52240
(319) 351-8523
Specialty: G
Resume Service

Office Manager
Perfect Page
2211 S 58th St
Lincoln, NE 68506
(402) 486-1201
Specialty: G
Resume Service

Office Manager
Personnel Professionals
2205 Camanche Av
Clinton, IA 52732
(319) 242-1078
Specialty: G
Resume Service

Resume Preparation Services

Office Manager
Phillips Secretarial Svc
2903 Gary Ave
Dodge City, KS 67801
(316) 225-3304
Specialty: G
Resume Service

Office Manager
Plaza Printers
6762 Douglas Avenue
Urbandale, IA 50322
(515) 278-4695
Specialty: G
Resume Service

Office Manager
Plus Two
312 6th Avenue SW
Aberdeen, SD 57401
(605) 226-2133
Specialty: G
Resume Service

Office Manager
Preference Personnel
1351 Page Dr SW
Fargo, ND 58103
(701) 293-6905
Specialty: G
Resume Service

Office Manager
Printed Word
1906 S Broadway Blvd
Salina, KS 67401
(913) 823-6557
Specialty: G
Resume Service

Office Manager
Printing Plus
1800 NW 86th Street
Clive, IA 50325
(515) 240-2950
Specialty: G
Resume Service

Office Manager
Professional Advantage
444 Badgerow Building
622 4th Street
Sioux City, IA 51101
(712) 252-4110
(800) 594-9446
Specialty: Resumes, Cover Letter, Reference Sheets
Resume Service

Office Manager
Professional Resume
852 Middle Road
Bettendorf, IA 52722
(319) 359-6515
Specialty: G
Resume Service

Office Manager
Professional Resume/Typing
42nd & Center Mall-Suite 123
Omaha, NE 68105
(402) 345-2425
Specialty: G
Resume Service

Office Manager
Quality Quick Print
37 1st Ave W
Dickinson, ND 58601
(701) 225-4070
Specialty: G
Resume Service

Elizabeth J Axnix, CPRW
Quality Word Processing
329 E Court Street
Iowa City, IA 52240-4914
(800) 359-7822
(319) 354-7822 FAX
Specialty: Same Day Fax &
Fedex Service Available
Member Professional Association
of Resume Writers
Resume Preparation Service

Office Manager
Raymond Communications
Custom Resumes
1309 Harlan Drive
Bellevue, NE 68005
(402) 291-1720
Specialty: G
Resume

Office Manager
Resumax
815 Saint Joseph Street
Rapid City, SD 57701
(605) 348-5578
Specialty: G
Resume Service

Office Manager
Resume Expert Systems
10500 Barkley St Ste 225
Shawnee Mission, KS 66212
(913) 381-4484
Specialty: G
Resume Service

Office Manager
Resume Inc
3020 N 102 St
Omaha, NE 68134
(402) 571-5522
Specialty: G
Resume Service

Office Manager
Resume Service
343 Colorado St
Manhattan, KS 66502
(913) 537-7294
Specialty: G
Resume Service

Office Manager
Resume' Svcs
231 Cherokee St
Leavenworth, KS 66048
(913) 682-1884
Specialty: G
Resume Service

Office Manager
Resumes Reports Etc
2316 S Stephen Avenue
Sioux Falls, SD 57103
(605) 371-3725
Specialty: G
Resume Service

Office Manager
Resumes Unlimited
Arbor & Hyland
Ames, IA 50010
(515) 292-3865
Specialty: G
Resume Service

Office Manager
Secretarial Support Services
7391 Pacific
Omaha, NE 68108
(402) 397-7888
Specialty: G
Resume Service

Office Manager
Shafer Resume Svc
512 Black Bldg
Fargo, ND 58102
(701) 237-9495
Specialty: G
Resume Service

Office Manager
Speedi-Graphics
1716 Avenue A
Scottsbluff, NE 69361
(308) 632-2425
Specialty: G
Resume Service

Office Manager
Spence Ewing & Associates
218 6 Avenue Ste 420
Des Moines, IA 50309
(515) 283-2473
Specialty: G
Resume Service

Office Manager
Technigraphics
Plaza Centre One Ste 20
Iowa City, IA 52240
(319) 354-5950
Specialty: G
Resume Service

Lori S McCormick, Owner
The Bottom Line
1102 Park Ave
Muscatine, IA 52761
(319) 263-6924
(319) 264-8406 FAX
Specialty: Word Processing, Laser Printing
Resume Preparation Service

Twila F Deahl, Owner
The Career Connection
1621 S University Drive Ste 215
Fargo, ND 58103
(701) 232-4614
(701) 241-9822 FAX
Specialty: C,E,F,M
Resume Preparation Service

Office Manager
The Office Alternative
3818 S Western Avenue
Sioux Falls, SD 57105
(605) 332-3711
Specialty: Entry Level to Executive
Resume Service

Office Manager
The Office Helpers
8525 Douglas Av
Omega Plaza Suite 39
Urbandale, IA 50322
(515) 270-2087
Specialty: G
Resume Service

Office Manager
The Printing Station
1023 Grand Ave
Des Moines, IA 50309
(515) 243-8144
Specialty: Professional Resume Packages Available
Resume Service

Office Manager
The Right Answer
1705 2nd Av Suite 100
Rock Island, IL 61201
(309) 793-4055
Specialty: G
Resume Service

Linda Morton, Owner
Transcriptions
1012 Massachusetts Street
Suite 202
Lawrence, KS 66044
(913) 842-4619
(913) 842-2846 FAX
Specialty: Resume Writing/Consulting
Resume Preparation Service

Office Manager
WEE Print & Copy
5785 Merle Hay Rd
Johnston, IA 50131
(515) 276-8501
Specialty: G
Resume Service

Office Manager
Word Merchants
102 S Main Street
Council Bluffs, IA 51503
(712) 322-2546
Specialty: G
Resume Service

Cyndi Saxon, Owner
Word Worx
612 E Douglas Ave
Wichita, KS 67202
(316) 265-9679
(316) 265-9706 FAX
Specialty: Laser Printing, ASCII Text File, Special Rates Updates
Resume Prepartion Service

Office Manager
Word Pros
522 7th Street Ste 206
Rapid City, SD 57701
(605) 342-0277
Specialty: G
Resume Service

Office Manager
Words Etc
1637 P St
Lincoln, NE 68508
(402) 476-2039
Specialty: G
Resume Service

Office Manager
Word Wizard
725 Memorial Hwy
Bismarck, ND 58504
(701) 222-3499
Specialty: G
Resume Service

Office Manager
Wordsworth
605 E 19th St N
Newton, IA 50208
(515) 792-1661
Specialty: G
Resume Service

Office Manager
Word Works
216 Main Street
Wayne, NE 68787
(402) 375-3729
Specialty: G
Resume Service

Office Manager
X-Pertise Personnel Inc
1854 Fuller Road
West Des Moines, IA 50265
(515) 225-7125
Specialty: G
Resume Service

Susan R Kelly, Program Director
YWCA Career Assistance Network
225 SW 12th Street
Topeka, KS 66612
(913) 232-8265
(913) 233-4867 FAX
Specialty: C,G,M
Resume Preparation Service

Office Manager
Zephyr Copies
124 E Washington St
Iowa City, IA 52240
(319) 351-3500
Specialty: G
Resume Service

Office Manager
Zip Instant Print
709 Main St
Keokuk, IA 52632
(319) 524-5333
Specialty: G
Resume Service

Office Manager
Zip Print & Advertising Co
Hwy 5 S
Albia, IA 52531
(515) 932-7949
Specialty: G
Resume Service

NET-RESEARCH PLACEMENT FIRM CONTACT FORM

Firm Name: _____

Address: _____

City: _____

State: _____ Zip: _____

Phone: (_____) _____

FAX: (_____) _____

Recruiter: _____

Specialty: _____

CONTACT LOG

	DATE	COMMENTS
1		
2		
3		
4		
5		

INTERVIEWS ARRANGED

DATE	TIME	COMPANY	CONTACT

Feel Free to copy this form

270 JOB SEEKERS SOURCE BOOK

NET-RESEARCH HIRING COMPANY CONTACT FORM

Firm Name: _____

Address: _____

City: _____

State: _____ Zip: _____

Phone: (_____) _____

FAX: (_____) _____

Position: _____

Salary: _____

BENEFITS SUMMARY

BENEFIT	Y/N	COMMENTS
Medical		
Dental		
Vacation		
Insurance		
Parking		
Business Car		
Other		

INTERVIEWS ARRANGED

DATE	TIME	CONTACT	COMMENTS

Feel Free to copy this form

READER FEEDBACK FORM

We would like to make the next edition of the "*Plains States Job Seekers SourceBook*" even better than this one. You, our readers and the users of this source book can help use with your comments and suggestions. Here is your opportunity to tell us what we're doing right and what we're doing wrong. So, please take a minute of your time and complete this form to:

- Tell us how we can make our next edition of the "*Plains States Job Seekers SourceBook*" more helpful;

- Tell us about any changes we should make to any entries; and

- Let us know of any useful job sources that we have overlooked.

If you run out of space, just attach another sheet. Please send your comments to: Net-Research, 16731 East Iliff, Suite B-183, Aurora, Colorado 80013. We must hear from you by **May 31, 1994** to include your suggestions in our next edition.

Thanks for your help to make our source books better.

Donald D. Walker

Comments and Suggestions:

_____

_____

_____

(More room available on the reverse side)

Comments & Suggestions (Continued)

_____
_____
_____
_____
_____
_____
_____
_____
_____
_____
_____
_____
_____
_____
_____
_____
_____
_____
_____

Purely Optional: Please include you name, address, and evening phone number in case we need to reach you for more information.

NET-RESEARCH SOURCEBOOK ORDER FORM

To obtain additional copies of this or other Net-Research Job Seekers SourceBooks, complete and return this order form. Your order will be shipped within 14 days or when published).

ORDER FORM BK-2: (* = Available Summer 1993)

	Job Seekers SourceBook	Price x Copies =	Total
___	Chicago & Illinois	$ 13.95 _____	$ _____
___	Boston & New England	$ 13.95 _____	$ _____
___	LA & Southern Calif.	$ 14.95 _____	$ _____
___	Pacific Northwest	$ 14.95 _____	$ _____
___	Dallas & The South West	$ 14.95 _____	$ _____
___	Southern States	$ 13.95 _____	$ _____
___	Ohio Valley	$ 14.95 _____	$ _____
___	Mid-Atlantic	$ 14.95 _____	$ _____
___	Southern Atlantic Coast	$ 14.95 _____	$ _____
___	Plains States	$ 13.95 _____	$ _____
___	Mountain States	$ 13.95 _____	$ _____
___	New York/New Jersey	$ 14.95 _____	$ _____
___	Northern Great Lakes	$ 14.95 _____	$ _____
___	**Entire set of Source Books**	**$162.50** _____	$ _____

Shipping and Handling (1st Copy) $ 3.00
Additional Copies = Number of copies X $1.00 = _____

Total Bill: $ _____

Payment Method Preferred: ____ Check Enclosed ____ VISA/MC

Card Number: _____

Expiration Date: _____

Signature Required: _____

Send Order To: (Please Print Clearly)

Name: _____

Address: _____

City: _____ St. _____ Zip: _____

Return this form to:
Net-Research, 16731 East Iliff, Suite B-183, Aurora, CO. 80113

NET-RESEARCH CONTACT SERVICE ORDER FORM

To assist our readers to quickly contact employment agencies and executive recruiters that serve particular specialties, Net-Research provides the following service: Resume and cover letter typing, 1st Class mail of these materials to selective firms by specialty and geographic area. 20 copies of the resume, a copy of the cover letter, and a list of all agencies or recruiters contacted is returned to purchaser via 2-day mail. To take advantage of this offer, complete and return this order form. Your order will be shipped within 14 days.

ORDER FORM CS-2:   (* = Available Summer 1993)

Job Seekers SourceBook Regions
- ___ Chicago & Illinois
- ___ Boston & New England
- ___ LA & Southern Calif.
- ___ Pacific Northwest
- ___ Dallas & The South West
- ___ * Southern States
- ___ Ohio Valley
- ___ Mid-Atlantic
- ___ Southern Atlantic Coast
- ___ * Plains States
- ___ * Mountain States
- ___ * New York/New Jersey
- ___ Northern Great Lakes

Type Firm to Contact
- ___ Employment Agency
- ___ Executive Search Firm
- ___ Both

Specific Specialties
_____
_____

Color of Bond Paper
- ___ Light Blue
- ___ Ivory
- ___ Light Gray

Base price (twenty firms contacted) $ 49.90
(Includes all shipping and handling, plus 20 copies of the resume returned to purchaser)
Additional firms contacted ($1.50 each) X _____ = _____

Total Bill: $ _____

Payment Method Preferred: ___ Check Enclosed   ___ VISA/MC

Card Number: _____

Expiration Date: _____

Signature Required: _____

Send Order To: (Please Print Clearly)   (Enclose readable resume and cover letter text) Cover letter limited to one page, resume to two)

Name: _____

Address: _____

City: _____ St._____ Zip:_____

Return form to: Net-Research, 16731 East Iliff, Suite B-183, Aurora, CO. 80013

275

NET-RESEARCH DATABASE ORDER FORM

The entries contained within each Source Book can also be obtained on a diskette, which comes with **free** software that allows the user access by: specialty, type firm, zip codes, or telephone area codes. To obtain database copies of this or other Net-Research Source Books, complete and return this order form. Your order will be shipped within 14 days.

ORDER FORM DB-2: (* = Available Summer 1993)

		Job Seekers SourceBook	Price x	Copies =	Total
	___	Chicago & Illinois	$ 24.95	_____	$ _____
	___	Boston & New England	$ 24.95	_____	$ _____
	___	LA & Southern Calif.	$ 24.95	_____	$ _____
	___	Pacific Northwest	$ 24.95	_____	$ _____
	___	Dallas & The South West	$ 24.95	_____	$ _____
*	___	Southern States	$ 24.95	_____	$ _____
	___	Ohio Valley	$ 24.95	_____	$ _____
	___	Mid-Atlantic	$ 24.95	_____	$ _____
	___	Southern Atlantic Coast	$ 24.95	_____	$ _____
*	___	Plains States	$ 24.95	_____	$ _____
	___	Mountain States	$ 24.95	_____	$ _____
	___	New York/New Jersey	$ 24.95	_____	$ _____
	___	Northern Great Lakes	$ 24.95	_____	$ _____
	___	**Entire set of databases**	**$275.00**	_____	$ _____

Shipping and Handling (1st Copy) $ 3.00
Additional Copies = Number of copies X $1.00   = _____

Total Bill: $ _____

<u>Payment Method Preferred:</u> ____ Check Enclosed ____ VISA/MC

Card Number: _____

Expiration Date: _____

Signature Required: _____

Send Order To: (Please Print Clearly)

Name: _____

Address: _____

City: _____ St. _____ Zip: _____

Return form to: Net-Research, 16731 East Iliff, Suite B-183, Aurora, CO. 80013

NET-RESEARCH WORD PROCESSING ORDER FORM

The entries contained within each Source Book can also be obtained on a diskette as a WordPerfect "Mail Merge" file. This allows the user to quickly generate cover letters using WordPerfect. To obtain copies of this or other Net-Research Source Books in WordPerfect "Mail Merge" format, complete and return this order form. Your order will be shipped within 14 days.

ORDER FORM MM-2:   (* = Available Summer 1993)

	Job Seekers SourceBook	Price	x Copies =	Total
___	Chicago & Illinois	$ 24.95	___	$ ___
___	Boston & New England	$ 24.95	___	$ ___
___	LA & Southern Calif.	$ 24.95	___	$ ___
___	Pacific Northwest	$ 24.95	___	$ ___
___	Dallas & The South West	$ 24.95	___	$ ___
___ *	Southern States	$ 24.95	___	$ ___
___	Ohio Valley	$ 24.95	___	$ ___
___	Mid-Atlantic	$ 24.95	___	$ ___
___	Southern Atlantic Coast	$ 24.95	___	$ ___
___	Plains States	$ 24.95	___	$ ___
___ *	Mountain States	$ 24.95	___	$ ___
___	New York/New Jersey	$ 24.95	___	$ ___
___	Northern Great Lakes	$ 24.95	___	$ ___
___	**Entire set of databases**	**$275.00**	___	$ ___

Shipping and Handling (1st Copy) $ 3.00
Additional Copies = Number of copies X $1.00   = ___

Total Bill: $ ___

Payment Method Preferred: ___ Check Enclosed   ___ VISA/MC

Card Number: _____

Expiration Date: _____

Signature Required: _____

Send Order To: (Please Print Clearly)

Name: _____

Address: _____

City: _____ St. _____ Zip: _____

Return form to: Net-Research, 16731 East Iliff, Suite B-183, Aurora, CO. 80013